IRON CHEF CHEN'S KNOCKOUT CHINESE

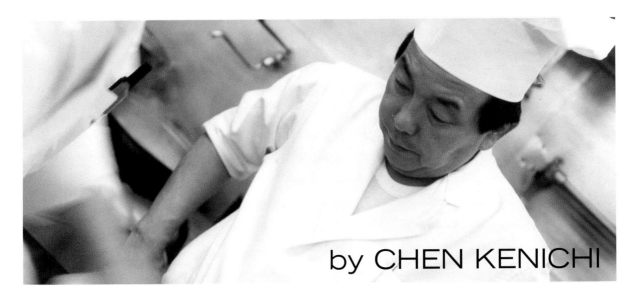

by CHEN KENICHI

VERTICAL.

Contents

Great for appetizers or snacks, or as a fancy treat with your favorite beer.

Stir-fried Broad Beans with Pickled Cabbage

Ingredients (serves 4)
7 oz (200 g) broad beans, shelled
1 3/4 oz (50 g) pickled cabbage (*xue cai*)
4" (10 cm) stalk bunching onion
   (or green onion or leek)
2 Tbsp vegetable oil
1 Tbsp sesame oil
A: dash each sugar, salt and pepper

1. Boil broad beans and chill in ice water. Peel off skins. Finely chop pickled cabbage and mince bunching onion (or green onion).
2. Heat oil in a pan and sauté pickled cabbage. Add sesame oil and broad beans, stir-fry briefly and add mixture A. Sauté, mixing occasionally. Add bunching onion, mix quickly and turn off heat.

Easy, tasty, and good if served cold, too.
I like this dish with a beer on a hot summer day.

Pounded Cucumber with Dried Shrimp

Pound cucumbers well. It makes it easier to remove the watery seeds and draw out the flavor.

Ingredients (serves 4)
2 cucumbers
1/2 tsp salt
1 oz (30 g) dried shrimp
4" (10 cm) bunching onion
  (or green onion or leek)
1 tsp each vegetable and sesame oil
A ┌ 2 tsp Doubanjiang
  │   (Chinese chili paste)
  └ Dash sugar

1. Quarter cucumbers lengthwise. Place face down and pound with flat of knife, then scrape off seeds with the blade. Cut pounded cucumbers into 1 1/4" (3 cm) pieces, then rub with salt. Let sit for 20 min. to draw out moisture.

2. Soak dried shrimp in water to reconstitute, then chop. Mince bunching onion.

3. Heat both oils in a wok, add shrimp and mixture A and sauté lightly. Wipe off moisture from cucumbers and add to wok. Add bunching onion and stir-fry briskly.

TIP: Pounding cucumbers with a knife makes it easier to scrape off the seeds and allows for better flavor absorption.

Pound the quartered cucumbers with the flat of the knife. This loosens the seeds.

Turn cucumber over and scrape off the seeds with the blade of the knife. They should come right off.

**I just love tasty octopus rings.
You can use the tentacle too—just cut it
into rounds and fry.**

Fried Octopus Rings

Ingredients (serves 4)
4 1/4 oz (120 g) boiled octopus rings
   (Or sub. calamari)
Batter:
  1 egg
  1/4 C water
  3 1/2 oz (100 g) flour
  1 3/4 oz (50 g) potato
    (or corn) starch
  1 Tbsp baking powder
  Dash salt
  1 Tbsp vegetable oil
  2 Tbsp parsley, minced
Oil, for deep-frying

1. Make batter. Crack egg into
a bowl and add water. Add flour,
starch, and baking powder. Mix
well by hand. Add salt and oil and
mix until sticky. Add parsley and mix.
2. Pat octopus tentacle rings
thoroughly dry and coat with corn-
starch. Dip in batter and fry gradually at low frying heat (300 to 320°F
(150 to 160°C)), occasionally turning
over.

TIP: You can use the leftover boiled
tentacles by turning them into a
simple dressed dish.

Thoroughly mix
the batter. The
starch makes
the batter stick
to the octopus.
Then fry it up as
soon as you can.

White Fish Sashimi

This recipe works well with any white meat fish, like flounder, perch or sea bream. Add sauce, mix well, and enjoy.

Ingredients (serves 4)
7 oz (200 g) sushi-grade white fish
6 to 7 wonton skins
Oil for deep-frying
4 Tbsp peanuts
Daikon, for garnish
4 radishes
4 green *shiso* leaves (or basil or mint)
Goji berries, to taste
Roasted white sesame seeds, to taste
Sauce:
⌐ 4 Tbsp peanut oil
  4 Tbsp soy sauce
∟ Dash sake
Dash sugar

1. Thinly slice fish. Fan out on a dish.
2. Deep-fry wonton skins and break into small pieces. Chop peanuts. Finely slice daikon and radishes and julienne *shiso* leaves.
3. Arrange the ingredients of step 2 on top of fish. Dress with goji berries and roasted sesame seeds. Combine sauce ingredients and pour on just before serving.

Cut fish by laying knife flat and pulling it towards you. Aim for the thickness of sashimi. You should be able to see through the slices.

Steamed Shrimp with Garlic

Ingredients (serves 4)
8 *kuruma* shrimp (or jumbo shrimp)
2 Tbsp diced garlic
2 Tbsp vegetable oil
A ⌈ 2 tsp potato (or corn) starch
  ⌊ Dash each sugar and salt
Chopped spring onions (or scallions) for garnish
Dash sesame oil

1. Slice shrimp along the back, cut open, and devein. Press lightly to flatten using the flat of a knife.
2. Rinse garlic lightly, squeeze dry, and fry in oil until lightly browned. Combine with mixture A and spoon onto flattened shrimp.
3. Steam shrimp over high heat for 4 to 5 minutes, serve, and sprinkle with spring onions. Heat sesame oil and add to dish for the finishing touch.

It's easy to devein the shrimp after cutting them open.
If you want, leave the heads on as an extra treat.

Coating the flattened shrimp with seasoned garlic is easier with a spoon.

Pork Shabu-Shabu with Sichuan Sauce

Ingredients (serves 4)
200 g (7oz) thinly sliced pork
Dash salt and sesame oil
4 Belgian endive leaves
2 radishes
1 cucumber
Sauce:
  ⌈ 2 Tbsp *tianjiangyou* (sweet soy
  │   sauce. See Reference Guide)
  │ 2 Tbsp soy sauce
  │ 1/2 Tbsp rice vinegar
  │ 2 tsp grated garlic
  ⌊ 1 tsp sesame oil
Dash chili oil

This technique of parboiling pork is called *shabu-shabu*.

1. Cut endive into bite-size pieces. Slice cucumber and radishes into thin rounds.
2. Bring ample water for dipping to a boil in a large wok. Swish thin pork slices in boiling water one by one just long enough to lightly brown. Drain water and season with salt and sesame oil. Let cool and cut into bite-size pieces.
3. Arrange pork and vegetables on a dish and top with sauce. Finish with a dash of chili oil.

Look for pork sold pre-cut into thin slices. I like a strong garlic flavor for this dish.

Savory Stir-fried Oysters

Dry oysters thoroughly and coat with plenty of starch. That's the key to making them crispy on the outside and juicy on the inside.

Ingredients (serves 4)
10 1/2 oz (300 g) oysters, shelled
Potato (or corn) starch
Oil, for deep-frying
4" (10 cm) bunching onion
    (or green onion)
2 Tbsp vegetable oil
A ⌐ 1 Tbsp minced garlic
    1 Tbsp minced *zha cai*
        (Sichuan vegetable)
    1 Tbsp minced fermented
        black beans (*douchi*)
    1 tsp seven-spice (or cayenne)
        powder
B ⌐ 1 Tbsp sake
    3/4 C (80 ml) soup stock
    1 tsp sugar
    1 tsp soy sauce
1 tsp starch paste
    (see Reference Guide)
Dash sesame oil

1. Rinse oysters and pat thoroughly dry. Coat each well with starch. Mince bunching onion.

2. Heat frying oil to 340 to 355°F (170 to 180°C) and drop in oysters one by one. Fry until crispy. Set fried oysters aside and drain oil.

3. Add 2 Tbsp oil to wok and stir-fry mixture A until fragrant. Add mixture B and mix well. Add fried oysters, stirring briskly to coat. Sprinkle on minced bunching onion and add starch paste to thicken sauce. Finish with sesame oil.

Wipe oysters thoroughly dry by placing between two paper towels and gently pressing.

Be careful not to burn garlic, *zha cai* or black beans when stir-frying. Cook just until fragrant.

Use the backside of a ladle to mix oysters in sauce quickly. Carefully avoid breaking up the crispy coating.

Grilled King Trumpet Mushrooms with Sesame Dressing

Ingredients (serves 4)
4 to 5 king trumpet mushrooms
Potato (or corn) starch
2 3/4 oz (80 g) shelled shrimp
Dash each salt and pepper
1 oz (30 g) cashew nuts, chopped
Daikon and cucumber, for garnish
2 Tbsp vegetable oil
Sesame dressing:
  1 tsp grated ginger
  1/2 tsp grated garlic
  1 1/2 Tbsp Chinese sesame paste
  1/2 tsp Doubanjiang
    (Chinese chili paste)
  1/2 tsp chili oil
  1 Tbsp sugar
  1 tsp rice vinegar
  2 1/2 Tbsp soy sauce

**King trumpet mushrooms prepared this way look and taste like abalone.
You can enjoy a luxurious experience without making your wallet cry.**

1. Slice off stem ends of king trumpet mushrooms. Cut lengthwise into about 1/5" (5 mm) slices and boil briefly. Pat dry and coat one side with starch.

2. Cut up shrimp then chop into a fine paste. Season with salt and pepper. Chop cashew nuts coarsely. Julienne daikon and cucumber.

3. Sandwich the shrimp paste between two mushroom slices, starch-coated sides facing in. Sprinkle with cashew nuts. Heat vegetable oil in a wok and cook mushrooms, cut into bite-size pieces, and arrange on a dish. Add daikon and cucumber garnish and sesame dressing.

TIP: When adding cashew nuts, press in gently to prevent them from falling off when frying.

Octopus with Spring Onion Sauce

Cooking the manly way, with an open flame. This dish goes great with cold sake.

Ingredients (serves 4)
5 1/4 oz (150 g) raw octopus
Onion sauce:
- 1 bunch spring onions
  (or scallions)
- 1 Tbsp minced ginger
- 1/2 tsp ground Sichuan pepper
  (*hua jiao fen*)
- 2 Tbsp vegetable oil
- 1 Tbsp sesame oil
- Dash sugar
- 1/4 tsp salt

1. Cut octopus into 1/4" (5 mm) slices, rinse in ice water, and pat dry. Arrange on a metal baking dish coated with oil and lightly char surface with a cooking torch.
2. Mince spring onions. Mix both oils, sugar, and salt. Add onions and remaining sauce ingredients. Pour over toasted octopus.

TIP: You can use a broiler if you don't have a torch. *Hua jiao fen* is a common spice in China, and is more fragrant than black pepper. If you can't find Sichuan pepper in your local store, you can substitute black pepper or Japanese (*sansho*) pepper.

A cooking torch is a tricky thing. Pass the flame over octopus just long enough to char it lightly. Be careful not to burn it.

Chop spring onions and scrape into a pile, then chop finely with the knife vertical then horizontal. This allows you to mince chives evenly and quickly.

Tofu Custard with Century Egg

Ingredients (serves 4)
1 block firm tofu
1 *pidang* (preserved duck egg, aka century egg)
2/3 oz (20 g) dried shrimp, reconstituted
1/3 oz (10 g) *zha cai* (Sichuan vegetable)
A ┌ 1/4 tsp salt
  │ 1 tsp soy sauce
  │ 2 tsp potato (or corn) starch
  └ 1 tsp sesame oil
Sauce: 2 Tbsp each sesame oil and soy sauce
Spring onions (or scallions), to taste

1. Drain tofu and mash with the flat of a knife. Place mashed tofu in a bowl. Peel *pidang* and chop into small pieces. Mince reconstituted shrimp and *zha cai* and add to mashed tofu together with *pidang*.

2. Add mixture A to tofu and mix quickly. Transfer tofu mixture to a small bowl lined with plastic film and smooth the top flat. Place this bowl in a steamer and steam over medium heat for 20 minutes.

3. Remove steamed tofu by flipping upside down, cut into four large chunks, and let cool. Arrange tofu on a plate. Combine sauce ingredients in a wok, heat, and sprinkle over tofu. Garnish with minced spring onions.

Press down on the tofu with a knife to mash it all at once. A Chinese broad-bladed knife comes in handy.

Add chopped *pidang*, dried shrimp, and *zha cai* to the mashed tofu one by one.

Lining the bowl with plastic wrap makes it easy to extract the steamed tofu. Cut tofu while hot, but wait to add sauce 'til after it cools.

Mash tofu, add ingredients, steam it, cool it, then add sauce. More complicated than it looks, huh? But that's what makes it taste so good.

My brother, who lives in Hong Kong, made this when he visited me in Japan. Just coat and broil. Simple, but tasty.

Honey Broiled Chicken Wings

Ingredients (serves 4)
12 chicken wings
1/3 tsp salt
A ⌐ 1 tsp rice vinegar
| 1 tsp soy sauce
| 1 Tbsp honey
└ 1 Tbsp sake
Vegetable oil
Lemon, to taste

1. Place chicken wings in a bowl, sprinkle on salt and rub in. Add mixture A, pressing in thoroughly. Let sit and allow flavor to absorb for 20 to 30 minutes.
2. Line toaster oven tray with aluminum foil and coat with oil. Arrange wings on top of the foil. Brush wings with leftover seasoning liquid 2 or 3 times while broiling. Broil for about 20 minutes until well browned. Add freshly squeezed lemon juice before serving.

It's best to use your hands to press the flavor in, as though you are massaging the seasonings into the wings.

Quick Meals and Light Lunches

These noodle and donburi recipes make great satisfying meals for one.

Meaty miso and cool cucumbers

on top of piping hot noodles.

It's an irresistible combination of cool and hot.

Sauté ground pork well until good and crumbly. Then add shiitake and sauté together.

Sauté thoroughly at low heat after adding minced garlic, sweet noodle sauce, and Doubanjiang to bring out the flavor.

Add starch paste evenly, using a circular motion. Heat well, stirring briskly.

Top piping hot noodles with plenty of meaty miso. Add cucumbers and mix well as you eat.

Meaty Miso with Noodles

Ingredients (serves 1)
1 bundle soft Chinese noodles
Meaty miso:
- 3 1/2 oz (100 g) ground pork
- 2 shiitake mushrooms
- 2" (5 cm) bunching onion (or green onion)
- 1 Tbsp vegetable oil
- 1/2 tsp minced garlic
- 1 Tbsp sweet noodle sauce (*tianmianjiang*. Or Hoisin)
- 1 tsp Doubanjiang (Chinese chili paste)
- 3/4 C (180 ml) soup stock
- 1 tsp sugar
- 1 Tbsp sake
- 1 Tbsp soy sauce
- Dash pepper
- 2 Tbsp starch paste (see Reference Guide)
- 1 tsp sesame oil

1/2 cucumber

A
- 1 tsp sesame oil
- 2 tsp soy sauce
- 1 Tbsp soup stock

1. Make meaty miso first. Remove shiitake stems and dice coarsely. Mince bunching onion. Heat vegetable oil in a wok and sauté ground pork until browned and crumbled. Add shiitake and sauté.

2. Add minced garlic, sweet noodle sauce, and Doubanjiang. Sauté well, being careful not to burn. Add soup stock, pepper, and minced bunching onion. Thicken sauce by adding starch paste and finish with sesame oil.

3. Boil noodles and cut cucumbers into thin strips 2" (5 to 6 cm) long. Combine mixture A in a dish. Transfer hot noodles to dish and top with meaty miso and sliced cucumber.

Don't over-boil the noodles. Add a bit of broth before topping with piping hot sauce. Aralia buds can be replaced with other green vegetables.

Noodles in Sauce with White Fish

Ingredients (serves 1)
1 bundle soft Chinese noodles
3 1/2 oz (100 g) white fish
  (e.g. sea bream)
1 1/3 C soup stock
4" (10 cm) bunching onion
  (or green onion)
2 tsp minced ginger
1 tsp minced garlic
1 Tbsp minced celery
2 Tbsp vegetable oil
1 Tbsp Doubanjiang
  (Chinese chili paste)
A ⌐ 2 tsp soy sauce
  │ 1 Tbsp sake
  │ 1 tsp sugar
  │ Dash pepper
  │ 2 Tbsp starch paste
  └   (see Reference Guide)
B ⌐ 1 tsp rice vinegar
  │ 1/2 tsp soy sauce
  └ 1 tsp chili oil
2 to 3 aralia buds (*tara no me*)

1. Simmer fish in soup stock and cut into small pieces. Set stock aside.
2. Heat oil in a wok and sauté garlic, ginger and Doubanjiang at low heat, being careful not to burn. Add 1 1/4 C of stock from step 1 and stir. Add fish and celery, season with mixture A, and sprinkle on minced bunching onion. Thicken sauce with starch paste.
3. Make cross-cuts at the base of fresh aralia buds and blanch briefly in boiling water.
4. Combine mixture B and add 1 Tbsp of remaining stock together in a dish. Boil noodles briefly, just until tender, and add to dish. Top with sauce and garnish with blanched aralia buds.

The fish will be cooked again, so don't worry if it's a little raw after boiling. Cut finely.

Sauté Doubanjiang and savory ingredients like garlic before adding the fish-flavored stock.

Add fish and celery, flavor with seasonings, thicken the sauce with starch paste and it's done.

Pouring sauce on one side makes for a delectable presentation.

Let's look at this simple recipe step by step. First, fill a bowl with plenty of chopped spring onions.

Next, add all the seasonings. The order doesn't matter, but I start with vinegar and soy sauce.

Add the soup mix and any other condiments that came with the ramen.

The bowl is ready. Soy sauce adds a robust aroma, but may be omitted if you're worried about sodium intake.

Follow package instructions for boiling ramen, then add lightly beaten egg.

Heat just until the egg congeals and transfer noodles to bowl.

Finished! Don't forget to stir seasonings up from the bottom before eating.

Spicy and Sour Noodle Soup

Ingredients (serves 1)

1 package of your favorite instant ramen

3 to 4 spring onions (or scallions)

1 egg

A ⌈ 2 tsp rice vinegar
  | 1 tsp soy sauce
  | 1 Tbsp chili oil
  | Dash pepper
  └ 1/2 tsp sesame oil

1. Mince spring onions and place in a bowl. Add mixture A and instant ramen flavoring.

2. Boil ramen noodles in approximately 2 cups of water and gradually add lightly beaten egg in a circular motion. Cook just until egg congeals and turn off the heat. Transfer noodles and egg soup to bowl with seasonings. Stir well before eating.

TIP: It says just a "dash" of pepper, but I like a lot of pepper in this recipe.

This is an easy-to-make version of a popular spicy and sour soup from Sichuan. It's a great way to satisfy your stomach and taste buds without too much trouble.

Prepare *zha cai* and seasonings as you boil noodles, and add noodles while still hot.

Mix noodles right away and coat well. Transfer to a serving dish and enjoy.

Noodles with *Zha Cai*

Place ingredients in a bowl, add cooked noodles, and mix. Almost too easy, isn't it? Ah, but wait! Don't forget to add hot oil for the finishing touch.

Ingredients (serves 1)
1 bundle soft Chinese noodles
1/3 oz (10 g) *zha cai* (Sichuan vegetable)
A ┌2 tsp *tianjiangyou* (sweet soy sauce. See Reference Guide)
  └1 tsp each soy sauce and chili oil
2 Tbsp chopped spring onions (or scallions)
1 Tbsp each sesame oil and vegetable oil

1. Mince *zha cai* and place in a bowl. Add mixture A. Boil noodles and add to bowl, mixing quickly. Transfer to a serving dish.
2. Sprinkle on chopped spring onions, heat both oils over high heat in a wok, and pour evenly over noodles. Mix well before eating.

Buckwheat Noodles with Egg

This was my favorite after-school snack when I was little. I learned to make it by watching my father. It's a unique twist to use Japanese buckwheat noodles.

Ingredients (serves 1)

1 3/4 oz (50 g) Japanese buckwheat noodles (*soba*)
1 egg
A ⌐ Dash salt
  ⌐ 1/2 Tbsp sake
1 to 2 Tbsp vegetable oil
2 cabbage leaves
2" (5 cm) bunching onion
  (or green onion)
Dash minced ginger
1 1/4 C soup stock or water
B ⌐ 1/2 Tbsp sake
  [1/3 tsp salt
  ⌐ Dash pepper
Chopped spring onions
  (or scallions)
Cayenne pepper, to taste

1. Coarsely chop cabbage into bite-size pieces. Cut bunching onion diagonally into 1/3" (1 cm) slices. Boil soba noodles.

2. Whisk egg and add mixture A. Heat oil in a wok and add egg. Cook quickly just until egg congeals, then add soup stock or water. Mix together.

3. Add bunching onion, ginger and cabbage. Flavor with mixture B and simmer until cabbage is tender. Add boiled buckwheat noodles and transfer to a serving dish. Sprinkle on spring onions and cayenne pepper before consuming.

Add seasoned egg mixture to a heated wok all at once, cooking over high heat.

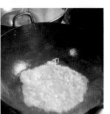
Stir egg briskly with broad strokes and cook just until congealed.

Add soup stock, or use water if there is no soup stock on hand.

Stir before adding additional ingredients, and then simmer.

Once the cabbage is tender, add boiled soba noodles.

Separate noodles with chopsticks and cook just enough to heat; don't overcook. Just pass the noodles through the soup.

Pork cutlet donburi is a common meal in Japan.

But I flavor mine with Doubanjiang, making it Sichuan-style.

Try it, you'll love the added spiciness.

Chen's Pork Cutlet Donburi

Ingredients (serves 1)
1 serving cooked rice
1 pork loin cutlet (3 1/2 oz (100 g))
A ┌ Pinch each salt and pepper
  └ 1 Tbsp sake
Flour, beaten egg, and panko
   (for coating)
Oil, for deep-frying
1/4 onion
2 eggs, lightly beaten
1 Tbsp vegetable oil
1/2 tsp sesame oil
1/2 Tbsp Doubanjiang
   (Chinese chili paste)
B ┌ 1/3 C soup stock
  │ 1 tsp sugar
  │ 1 Tbsp each sake and soy
  │   sauce
  │ Dash Japanese soup stock
  │   powder (see Reference
  └   Guide)

1.   Cut tendons and pound pork
lightly. Season with mixture A.
Coat with flour, beaten egg, and
panko bread crumbs (in that
order). Fry until crispy in 340°F
(170°C) oil and cut into bite-size
pieces.

2.   Thinly slice onion and sauté in
vegetable oil. Add sesame oil and
Doubanjiang. Add mixture B and
simmer at low heat until onions
are tender. Add fried pork cutlet
and simmer briefly.

3.   Pour lightly beaten egg in a
circular motion over simmered
cutlet. Heat until egg is half-
cooked. Slide egg and pork cutlet
topping onto hot rice in a serving
bowl.

Cut onions
against the grain
and sauté until
translucent.

Add seasonings
and simmer onions
at low heat until
tender.

Add fried pork
cutlet and simmer
briefly before
pouring in egg.

Simmer until
eggs are cooked.
I prefer my eggs
runny.

Slide pork mixture
over hot rice,
using a spatula to
keep everything
together.

Miso-Sautéed Pork Donburi

Ingredients (serves 1)
3 1/2 oz (100 g) thinly sliced
   pork belly
1 bunching onion
   (or green onion)
1 Tbsp vegetable oil
A ┌1 tsp grated garlic
  │ 2 tsp Doubanjiang
  │ (Chinese chili paste)
  │ 1 tsp sweet noodle sauce (*tian-*
  └ *mianjiang*. Or Hoisin sauce)
B ┌1 Tbsp sake
  │ 1 Tbsp soy sauce
  │ Dash sugar
  └Dash pepper

**This is a great dish for nights
you cook for yourself.
Cook pork until it's nice and crispy.
That's what makes it extra tasty.**

1. Cut pork into bite-size pieces.
Cut bunching onion diagonally into
1/4" (5 mm) slices.
2. Heat oil in a wok and cook pork
slowly at medium heat until crispy.
Add mixture A and stir. Add bunching onion and sauté until tender.
Add mixture B and stir-fry briskly.
Serve on top of hot rice.

TIP: When cooking pork, separate
and add each pork slice one by
one to keep them from sticking
together.

Add pork slices
one by one and
cook until crispy.
Use medium heat,
not high.

Add bunching
onions to the pork
and cook until
translucent.

Add seasonings
and stir-fry quickly,
being careful not
to burn.

Spicy Eggplant Donburi

Ingredients (serves 1)

1 serving cooked rice
1 large eggplant
Oil, for deep-frying
2 3/4 oz (80 g) ground pork
2 tsp ginger, minced
1 tsp garlic, minced
2" (5 cm) bunching onion
   (or green onion)
2 Tbsp vegetable oil
1 Tbsp Doubanjiang
   (Chinese chili paste)
1 tsp sweet noodle sauce
   (*tianmianjiang*. Or Hoisin sauce)
1/2 C (120 ml) soup stock
A ⌐ 2 tsp sake/ 2 tsp sugar
   | 1 tsp soy sauce
   └ Dash pepper
2 Tbsp starch paste
   (see Reference Guide)
B ⌐ 1/2 tsp rice vinegar
   └ Dash vegetable oil

1. Cut eggplant into large bite-size pieces. Fry in 355°F (180°C) oil.
2. Heat oil in a wok and sauté ground pork. Add ginger, garlic, Doubanjiang and sweet noodle sauce and stir-fry.
3. Add eggplant and soup stock to ground pork. Add mixture A and simmer briefly. Sprinkle in minced bunching onion and thicken sauce with starch paste. Finish with mixture B and serve on top of hot rice.

Sichuan-style spicy "mapo" meat sauce is pretty famous now in Japan. Maybe you've heard of it? It goes especially well with eggplant.

Mince *takanazuke*, cut pork, and add flavorings. Slice chili pepper into rounds. For super-spicy spaghetti, add an extra chili pepper.

Add pork to the heated oil. Break up the meat as you cook.

When pork is browned, add *takanazuke* and chili pepper and stir-fry well.

Spaghetti with Pork and *Takanazuke*

Spaghetti the Sichuan way—you'll be amazed at what a great combination chili peppers, pickled mustard greens and pork make. *Takanazuke* is salty, so be careful not to add too much extra salt.

Ingredients (serves 1)
3 1/2 oz (100 g) spaghetti
1 3/4 oz (50 g) *takanazuke* (pickled mustard greens. Or pickled cabbage)
3 1/2 oz (100 g) thinly sliced pork belly
A ┌Dash each salt and pepper
  │ 1 Tbsp sake
  │ 1 Tbsp starch paste
  │   (see Reference Guide)
  └ 1 tsp vegetable oil
1 red chili pepper
1 Tbsp vegetable oil
B ┌1 Tbsp bunching onion
  │   (or green onion), minced
  │ 1 tsp soy sauce
  └ 1 tsp sesame oil

1. Boil spaghetti. Mince *takanazuke* and cut pork into small bite-size pieces. Flavor with mixture A, mixing well. Remove seeds of chili pepper and slice into thin rounds.
2. Heat oil in a wok and sauté pork, keeping the meat from sticking together. Add chili pepper and minced *takanazuke* and stir-fry.
3. Add boiled spaghetti to the wok and stir. Add mixture B, mix quickly, and transfer to a serving dish.

Spicy Spaghetti with Broccoli

Ingredients (serves 1)
3 1/2 oz (100 g) spaghetti
1/2 stalk broccoli
1 clove garlic
3 to 4 Tbsp olive oil
1 tsp Doubanjiang
   (Chinese chili paste)
1 tsp fermented black beans
   (*douchi*), minced
Dash black pepper

1. Break up broccoli into clusters and cook in boiling water. Chop coarsely. Boil spaghetti at the same time. Pound garlic with flat of knife, then mince.
2. Sauté garlic in half of the olive oil, being careful not to burn. Add Doubanjiang and continue sautéing. Add broccoli and fermented black beans in that order and stir-fry.
3. Add remaining olive oil to broccoli and let sit briefly. Add 2 Tbsp of boiling liquid from spaghetti and the spaghetti noodles. Mix quickly. Add pepper for the finishing touch.

Those little black flecks are *douchi*. They may not look like much, but they add another dimension to this dish. The broccoli, by the way, should be cooked well until tender.

Boil broccoli then cut until the florets are all broken up.

Pound garlic with the flat of a knife. This brings out the aroma and makes it easy to mince.

Mince pounded garlic coarsely.

Use olive oil with spaghetti. Add Doubanjiang, broccoli, and fermented black beans.

Add spaghetti at the end, mix quickly, and serve.

TIP: Add the garlic to the olive oil before it gets too hot. If you burn the garlic, it turns bitter.

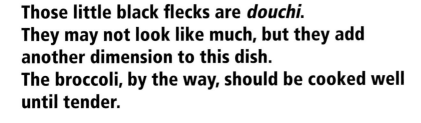

3 Creative Concoctions with Leftovers

Delicious hints on how to clear out your pantry without tossing everything into the trash can.

Crunchy Pickled Daikon

For a nice crunchy finish and a rich flavor, allow 2 to 3 days for drying and 2 to 3 days for marinating the daikon.

Ingredients (serves 4)
10 1/2 oz (300 g) daikon, peeled
Marinade:
- 20 grains Sichuan peppercorn (*hua jiao*)
- 3 red chili peppers
- 2/3 C (170 ml) *Shaoxing* wine (Chinese rice wine)
- 1/2 C water
- 1/2 Tbsp sugar
- 5 Tbsp soy sauce

1. Chop daikon into bite-size pieces of equal size. Spread out on a tray and let dry for 2 to 3 days. Remove seeds from chili peppers and shred.

2. Mix marinade ingredients together in a large bowl. Add dried daikon and mix well. Cover with plastic wrap and chill in the refrigerator for 2 to 3 days, allowing the flavor to absorb.

TIP: If you stir the daikon twice a day while it is pickling in the marinade, the flavor will absorb more evenly.

This is how the daikon should look after a few days. Soaking well-dried daikon in marinade with Sichuan peppercorn and red chili peppers makes for a delectable crunchy treat.

Stir-fried Daikon Peel

If you enjoy Japanese slow-cooked hot pots, you'll find this recipe is a great way to make use of the leftover daikon peels.

Ingredients (serves 4)
1 daikon peel
Daikon leaves
1/2 bunching onion
   (or green onion)
2 3/4 oz (80 g) shelled shrimp
A ⎡Dash each salt and pepper
   ⎢1/2 white of 1 egg
   ⎢2/3 Tbsp potato (or corn)
   ⎢   starch
   ⎣2 Tbsp vegetable oil
B ⎡1 Tbsp sake
   ⎢1 tsp soy sauce
   ⎢1/4 tsp salt
   ⎣Dash pepper
1 tsp sesame oil

1. Spread daikon peels on a tray and dry for one day. Dice peels into 1/3" (1 cm) pieces and slice daikon leaves into 1/3" (1 cm) pieces. Mince bunching onion.
2. Devein shrimp, cut into 1/3" (1 cm) pieces and coat thoroughly with mixture A.
3. Heat oil and stir-fry daikon peels. Add daikon leaves and stir-fry until lightly charred.
4. Add seasoned shrimp and continue stir-frying. Add mixture B, mix quickly and top with minced bunching onion and sesame oil.

TIP: This dish should be stir-fried slowly over medium-low heat.

Allowing the peels to dry for a day brings out the flavor and creates a scrumptious texture.

The leaves are another often-discarded ingredient. Add them after stir-frying the peels and cook until lightly charred. Then, add the shrimp.

Once all the seasonings have been added, stir-fry briskly while tossing all the ingredients in the wok.

Stir-fried Leftover Vegetables with Ground Pork

Ingredients (serves 4)
2 cabbage leaves
1 cucumber
2 3/4 oz (80 g) daikon
2 3/4 oz (80 g) carrot
A ⌈ 1 tsp salt
  ⌊ 4 Tbsp sake
5 1/4 oz (150 g) ground pork
2 red chili peppers
1/2 bunching onion (or green onion
   or leek)
2 Tbsp vegetable oil
B ⌈ 1 Tbsp sweet noodle sauce
  │   (*tianmianjiang*. Or Hoisin)
  │ 1 Tbsp each soy sauce and sake
  ⌊ Dash pepper
1 tsp sesame oil

1. Dice cabbage, cucumber, daikon and carrot into 1/4" (5 mm) pieces. Place in a bowl, add mixture A and mix well by hand. Press lightly with a weight for 20 to 30 min. Transfer to a sheet of cheesecloth and squeeze out excess moisture.

2. Deseed red chili peppers and cut into thin rounds.

3. Heat oil and sauté pork until crumbled. Add red chili peppers and mixture B and mix quickly. Add vegetables and stir-fry briskly at high heat, allowing moisture to evaporate. Finish with minced bunching onion and sesame oil.

Put vegetables in a large bowl and massage in salt and sake by hand to draw the moisture out.

Sauté pork until crumbly, add red chili peppers and then other seasonings.

Add vegetables all at once and mix quickly at high heat to burn off all the water.

This is the staff dinner back in the kitchen at the restaurant. When things are busy, we just throw the veggies in the food processor, stir-fry, and voilà! Instant dinner.

Grilled Pork with Bunching Onion

Ingredients (serves 4)
5 1/4 oz (150 g) grilled pork
1 3/4 oz (50 g) bunching onion
   (or green onion or leek)
A ┌ 1 tsp Tamari soy sauce
   │ 1 Tbsp sesame oil
   │ 1 tsp Doubanjiang
   │   (Chinese chili paste)
   └ Dash sugar

1. Cut grilled pork into strips 1/5 to 1/4" (4 to 5 mm) wide. Julienne bunching onion.
2. Combine mixture A in a bowl, add grilled pork and mix well. Add bunching onion and mix. Transfer to a dish.

Add pork to a bowl with pre-mixed seasonings and coat by stirring quickly.

Add thinly sliced bunching onion and mix. How simple!

A treat you can make while the kids are in the bath. Here's a way to reinvent last night's pork dish.

Octopus Legs with Sweet and Sour Sauce

Mix sauce thoroughly to dissolve sugar, pour it onto the crispy fried octopus, and eat right away.

Ingredients (serves 4)
8 3/4 oz (250 g) octopus legs
Potato (or corn) starch
Oil, for deep-frying
Sweet and Sour Sauce:
- 3 Tbsp sugar
- 2 Tbsp rice vinegar
- 4 Tbsp soy sauce
- 1 Tbsp ginger, grated
- 2 tsp sesame oil
- 6" (15 cm) bunching onion, minced
- Chopped spring onions (or scallions)

1. Cut octopus legs into bite-size pieces and coat with starch. Fry in 320°F (160°C) oil until crisp. Drain excess oil.
2. Mix ingredients for sauce thoroughly and pour over octopus.

Use a relatively low temperature to fry octopus and take it out as soon as the coating is crispy.

Stir-fried Bean Sprouts with Garlic Chives

Cut garlic chives into bite-size pieces. The bean sprouts are best when crispy, so use a well-heated wok and stir-fry quickly.

Ingredients (serves 4)
1 bundle garlic chives
1 pack bean sprouts
1 3/4 oz (50 g) squid *shiokara*
    (salted entrails)
2 Tbsp vegetable oil
Dash salt
1 Tbsp sesame oil

1. Cut garlic chives into 1" (2.5 cm) strips. Remove root ends of bean sprouts. Chop squid *shiokara* finely.

2. Heat oil in a wok and quickly stir-fry bean sprouts. Add squid *shiokara* and garlic chives, in that order, and sauté briskly. Add salt and finish with sesame oil.

Quickly stir-fry bean sprouts over high heat until coated with oil. Add squid *shiokara*.

Add garlic chives. Stir-fry briefly and season. High heat and a short cooking time keep the vegetables crisp.

Creamy Simmered Broccoli Stems

Ingredients (serves 4)
4 broccoli stems
4 crab legs, boiled and cut 2" pieces
1 cut swordfish (appx. 2 3/4 oz (80 g))
2 scallops
4 shelled shrimp
2 oz (60 g) cuttlefish
A ⌈ 1/4 tsp salt
    │ Dash pepper
    │ 1 tsp each sake and egg white
    └ 1 heaping Tbsp potato starch
Pinch dried wood ear mushroom
4" (10 cm) bunching onion (or leek)
1 nub ginger
Oil for deep-frying
2 Tbsp vegetable oil
1 C soup stock
B ⌈ 1 Tbsp sake
    │ Dash sugar
    │ 1/4 tsp salt
    └ Dash pepper
2 Tbsp starch paste (see Reference
    Guide)

1. Peel thick skin off broccoli using a small knife. Cut in half lengthwise and make several diagonal scores to facilitate cooking. Cut diagonally into 1/2" (1.5 cm) wide pieces.
2. Remove crab meat from shell. Cut swordfish into 4 slices. Cut scallops in half diagonally. Devein shrimp. Make shallow cuts on the surface of the squid and cut into thin slices.
3. Reconstitute mushrooms and cut into bite-size pieces. Cut bunching onion into 1/4" (1 cm) pieces.
4. Season seafood prepared in step 2 with mixture A.
5. Heat oil in a wok to 320°F (160°C) and fry broccoli. Drain oil and use the same wok to stir-fry seasoned seafood, spreading them out evenly over the surface of the wok. Set seafood aside.

6. Add 2 Tbsp of vegetable oil to the emptied wok and sauté bunching onion and grated ginger. Pour in soup stock and bring to a boil. Add fried broccoli, stir-fried seafood, and mushrooms. Let simmer briefly. Add mixture B and thicken sauce with starch paste.

The skin of the stems is tough and grainy, but the inside is tender. Use a small knife to peel the thick skin off.

When frying broccoli, just submerge briefly in hot oil. Frying brings out the color.

Peel off grainy fibers and cut in half lengthwise. Score on the bias to ensure tenderness.

Mix starch in thoroughly to thicken the sauce.

This dish is so good you might not wait for leftover broccoli stems. Better think of a way to use the leftover broccoli flowers instead. The seafood listed can be replaced with a pre-packaged seafood mix.

4

Chinese the Chen Way

These are recipes I inherited from my father, Chen Kenmin—please cook them with care.

When my dad first served this dish in Japan, it was too spicy for his customers.

However, it's now one of the signature dishes of our restaurant.

The numbing spice of *hua jiao* is the distinctive flavor of the Sichuan province.

Try to use the original ingredients; it's just not the real thing without them.

Genuine Mapo Tofu

Ingredients (serves 4)

1 block firm tofu
2 3/4 oz (80 g) ground pork
1 garlic sprout
2 Tbsp vegetable oil
1 heaping Tbsp Doubanjiang
  (Chinese chili paste)
1 tsp sweet noodle sauce (*tianmianjiang*)
2 tsp fermented black beans
  (*douchi*), minced
1 Tbsp cayenne pepper
1 Tbsp chili oil
3/4 C (180 ml) soup stock
A ⎡ 1 Tbsp sake
  ⎢ 1 tsp soy sauce
  ⎣ Dash salt
2 Tbsp starch paste (see Reference Guide)
2 Tbsp vegetable oil
1 tsp ground Sichuan pepper (*hua jiao fen*)

1. Cut tofu from the side into 2 halves of equal thickness. Dice halves into 1" (2 cm) cubes and boil in salted water until firm. Set aside. Mince the white part of garlic sprout and cut the green leaves into bite-size pieces.
2. Heat 2 Tbsp of oil in a wok and add ground pork. Cook at high heat until crispy and crumbled. Add Doubanjiang, sweet noodle sauce, black beans, cayenne, and half of the chili oil and stir-fry.
3. Drain water from tofu and add to sautéed meat mixture. Add soup stock and white part of garlic sprout. Simmer, mixing occasionally. Add mixture A and the remaining chili oil, gradually, to taste. Sprinkle in green part of garlic sprout.
4. Add starch paste and turn heat to medium. Stir slowly until sauce thickens, then add vegetable oil. Transfer to a serving dish.

TIP: Garlic sprouts are early-harvest garlic. They have a milder flavor than garlic cloves. You can use garlic cloves and scallions instead.

Use firm tofu. Don't forget to cut in half before dicing.

Next are the garlic sprout, sake, and seasonings. Add remaining chili oil gradually. Add leaves from garlic sprout last.

To keep the tofu from breaking apart when simmering, boil it in salted water until firm.

Stir in starch paste slowly and thoroughly, reducing heat to medium.

Make 2 or 3 lengthwise slices into the white part of garlic sprouts and slice into rounds.

Add oil and turn off heat. The oil makes the dish glisten. You can use sesame oil or Sichuan peppercorn oil, too.

This dish uses various seasonings characteristic of Sichuan cuisine. Place each spice into small dishes ahead of time.

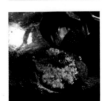

Grease the wok before sautéing. Cook ground pork until crumbly and crispy, then add Doubanjiang.

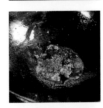

Doubanjiang is followed in quick succession by sweet noodle sauce, black beans, and cayenne pepper.

Leave half of chili oil for later. Stir-fry spices quickly to bring out aroma.

When ground pork and spices turn a dark brown color, add boiled tofu and soup stock.

This mild version of Mapo Tofu is great for kids
and people who don't like super-spicy foods.
Actually, the ingredients for this version are more luxurious.

Mild Mapo Tofu

Ingredients (serves 4)
1 block firm tofu
3 1/2 oz (100 g) beef thigh
A ⌐1 Tbsp sake
    1/2 tsp salt
    Dash pepper
    1 Tbsp lightly beaten egg
    └1 Tbsp potato (or corn) starch
4 Tbsp vegetable oil
1 Tbsp oyster sauce
3/4 C (180 ml) soup stock
B ⌐1 Tbsp each sake and soy sauce
    1 tsp sugar
    └Dash each salt and pepper
2 Tbsp starch paste
  (see Reference Guide)
2 spring onions (or scallions)

1. Wrap tofu in a paper towel to drain off water. Cut from side into 2 halves of equal thickness. Dice into large cubes.
2. Cut beef into 1/4" (5 mm) thick slices and make shallow cuts against the grain of the muscle. Slice into narrow strips and then mince. Add all ingredients of mixture A except for the starch and massage into meat by hand until flavor is well absorbed. Add starch and coat well.
3. Heat 2 Tbsp of oil in a wok, add beef and sauté. Add oyster sauce and continue sautéing. Pour in soup stock and add tofu. Season with mixture B and simmer, stirring gently, for 2 to 3 minutes.
4. Add starch paste and simmer, stirring occasionally, until sauce thickens. Sprinkle with onions and add remaining 2 Tbsp oil. Turn off heat.

TIP: If the meat is minced thoroughly it's so soft even a toddler could eat it. Maybe.

Cut tofu into large bite-size pieces. Use tofu as is, without boiling, for a soft finish.

Slice beef, make cuts against the grain, slice into strips, and mince. This is the way to make tough meat tender.

Use your hands to gently massage seasonings into beef.

For a deliciously juicy dish, massage flavor in like this, allowing seasonings to thoroughly absorb.

Sauté beef over medium heat until meat is mostly browned. Add oyster sauce.

Add tofu, soup stock, and other seasonings in rapid succession.

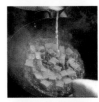
Simmer and stir gently, being careful not to break up tofu. Thicken sauce with starch paste.

Add onions and oil for a nice finish.

This dish is an old favorite in the Sichuan province
and is popular in Japan as well.
My father did a lot of experimenting before settling on this final version.
Simmered with ketchup, Chen's Chili Shrimp has
a deliciously mellow flavor.

Chen's Chili Shrimp

Ingredients (serves 4)
10 1/2 oz (300 g) shelled shrimp
A ┌ 1/4 tsp salt
  │ Dash pepper
  │ 1 egg white
  │ 1 heaping Tbsp potato
  └   (or corn) starch
1 3/4 oz (50 g) green peas (raw or frozen)
4" (10 cm) bunching onion
   (or green onion)
3 Tbsp vegetable oil
B ┌ 2 Tbsp vegetable oil
  │ 1 Tbsp Doubanjiang
  │   (Chinese chili paste)
  │ 3 Tbsp ketchup
  │ 1 tsp garlic, grated
  └ 1 Tbsp ginger, grated
C ┌ 1 C soup stock
  │ 1 Tbsp sake
  │ 2 tsp sugar
  └ Dash each salt and pepper
2 Tbsp starch paste
   (see Reference Guide)
1 egg (leftover from 1 Tbsp egg white
   listed above)
1/2 tsp rice vinegar

1. Rinse shrimp well, pat dry and devein.
Boil green peas, or if frozen, defrost.
Mince bunching onion.
2. Season shrimp with A ingredients,
adding in listed order and mixing well
by hand.
3. Heat 2 Tbsp oil in a wok and
quickly add shrimp. Sauté until surface
is cooked, rocking wok occasionally.
Flip and repeat on the other side. Set
shrimp aside.
4. Add B ingredients to wok in listed
order. Stir-fry well at low heat, being
careful not to burn. Stir in mixture C.
5. Add cooked shrimp to sauce and
sprinkle in green peas and minced
bunching onion. Thicken sauce with
starch paste. Pour in egg and stir lightly.
Finish with rice vinegar and 1 Tbsp oil
and turn off heat.

Shelled shrimp
should be rinsed
and patted
thoroughly dry
with a paper
towel.

Coat shrimp with
egg and starch
after seasoning
with salt and
pepper.

As always, sea-
soning should
be gently
massaged in by
hand.

Add each
shrimp quickly.
Cook until
crisped, rocking
wok to prevent
burning.

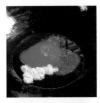

Set aside shrimp.
Add oil,
Doubanjiang,
ketchup, grated
ginger and garlic.

Turn heat down
to low and sim-
mer until fra-
grant. Be care-
ful not to burn
the seasonings.

Add soup and sake
and mix to evenly
distribute flavor.
Return shrimp to
wok and sprinkle
in green peas and
onion.

Thicken with
starch paste and
slowly pour in egg,
which gives the
sauce a mellow
flavor. Finish with
oil and rice vinegar.

On the rare occasions when my father was at home for dinner
and in a good mood, he would make this dish.
He used bacon instead of pork. Since his Japanese pronunciation
was bad, it sounded like "Miso Beer Can with Cabbage."

Miso Pork with Cabbage

Ingredients (serves 4)

7 oz (200 g) pork belly
3 cabbage leaves
1 red bell pepper
1 green bell pepper
1/2 bunching onion (or green onion)
2 Tbsp vegetable oil
A ┌ 1 Tbsp Doubanjiang (Chinese chili
    │   paste)
    │ 1 Tbsp sweet noodle sauce
    │   (*tianmianjian*g. Or Hoisin sauce)
    │ 1 tsp garlic, minced
    │ 1 tsp fermented black beans
    └   (*douchi*), minced
B ┌ 1 Tbsp sake
    └ 1 tsp soy sauce
1 Tbsp starch paste (see Reference Guide)

1. Cut pork belly in half. Cut each half into 1/8" (3 mm) thick pieces, then thinly slice into bite-size pieces.
2. Cut cabbage into similarly sized pieces, thinly slicing core. Remove stems and seeds from bell peppers and chop into chunks. Cut bunching onion diagonally into 1/4" (5 mm) thick slices.
3. Bring 4 C water to a boil and add 1 Tbsp oil and 1 tsp salt. Briefly boil cabbage and bell peppers, in that order. Drain water.
4. Heat oil in a wok and place pork slices in one by one. Don't overlap. Stir-fry over high heat. Once pork is lightly browned add onion, stir-fry, and add mixture A. Stir-fry well. Add cabbage, bell peppers, and mixture B and mix quickly to coat. Thicken sauce with starch paste.

The original recipe doesn't call for bell peppers, but they add color and nutrition, too.

Boil cabbage and bell peppers in water with oil and salt just until tender. Drain off water.

Stir-fry pork just long enough to lightly brown, then add bunching onion and seasonings.

Stir-fry briskly until fragrant.

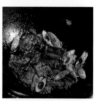

Add vegetables and stir-fry. Finish with sake and soy sauce, and add starch paste to thicken.

In the Sichuan province, Tan Tan Noodles were originally sold by street vendors, which is why they were served dry, as opposed to the popular soup-style version. The original did have ground pork though, which I omitted from this recipe for a lighter, more refreshing dish.

Sichuan-Style Tan Tan Noodles

Ingredients (serves 1)
1 bundle Chinese egg noodles
Topping:
- 2 Tbsp bunching onion (or green onion), minced
- 1 tsp *zha cai* (Sichuan vegetable), minced
- 1 Tbsp Chinese sesame paste
- 1 Tbsp soy sauce
- 1/2 tsp rice vinegar
- 1 Tbsp chili oil
- Dash cayenne pepper

1. Set aside some of the *zha cai* and minced bunching onion for use as garnish, and mix remainder together with other topping ingredients in a bowl.

2. Boil noodles and drain, reserving 2 Tbsp boiling liquid. Transfer noodles to bowl with topping ingredients. Add boiling liquid and mix.

3. Transfer to a dish and garnish with reserved *zha cai* and bunching onion. Add extra chili oil to taste.

TIP: Serve topping on individual dishes and add piping hot noodles just before eating. This allows each person to mix their own noodles.

Sauté pork thoroughly until crumbled. Add seasonings and mix well.

Add soy sauce and rice vinegar first, then add sesame paste, chili oil and green onion oil.

Add *zha cai* and bunching onion, stir, then pour in hot soup. Mix well, and add noodles.

Chen Kenmin-Style Tan Tan Noodles

It was my father who came up with the idea of turning Tan Tan Noodles into a noodle soup dish, since the dry seasoned noodles weren't very popular in Japan. He refused to eat his invention himself, though. Personally, I prefer this version.

Ingredients (serves 1)
1 bundle Chinese egg noodles
1 3/4 oz (50 g) ground pork
1/2 to 1 Tbsp vegetable oil
A ⌈ 1/2 Tbsp sweet noodle sauce
   (*tianmianjiang*. Or Hoisin)
   1 tsp sake
   1 tsp soy sauce
  ⌊ Dash pepper
1/4 bunch spinach
B ⌈ 1 tsp rice vinegar
   2 Tbsp soy sauce
   2 Tbsp Chinese sesame paste
   2 Tbsp chili oil
  ⌊ 1 tsp green onion oil
1 Tbsp *zha cai* (Sichuan
   vegetable), minced
2 Tbsp bunching onion, minced
1 1/4 C soup stock

1. Heat oil in a wok and cook ground pork until crumbled. Add mixture A and stir-fry briskly.
2. Boil spinach. Drain water and cut to 2" (5 cm) lengths.
3. Combine mixture B in a bowl, adding in the order listed. Add *zha cai* and bunching onion and stir together. Heat soup stock.
4. Cook noodles just until *al dente*, then set on a tray to drain. Pour hot soup into the bowl with mixture B, mix briefly, and transfer noodles to soup. Top with pork and spinach. Mix well before consuming.

TIP: Green onion oil is onion-infused lard. It rounds out the flavor of stir-fried vegetable dishes and soups. To make, use 17 1/2 oz (500 g) of lard, the stalk of 1 green onion, and 1 nub of minced ginger. Simmer all ingredients in a sauce pan over medium heat for approximately 10 minutes, stirring constantly. Remove onion and ginger and store lard in the fridge. It keeps for approximately 1 month.

In Japan, pan-fried gyoza dumplings are popular.

But in China, gyoza are usually boiled.

Try them piping hot and served with sweet and spicy sauce.

Boiled Dumplings

Ingredients (serves 4)
20 wonton skins
Filling:
- 4 oz (120 g) ground pork
- 1 tsp juice from grated ginger
- 1 Tbsp sake
- 1/3 tsp salt
- Dash pepper
- 4 Tbsp water
- 2 tsp potato (or corn) starch
- 1 tsp sesame oil

Sauce:
- 1 Tbsp ground garlic
- 2 tsp rice vinegar
- 3 Tbsp *tianjiangyou* (sweet soy sauce. See below)
- 3 Tbsp soy sauce
- 4 Tbsp Chinese sesame paste
- 1 Tbsp chili oil

2 bunches bok choy

1. Place ground pork in a bowl and add ginger juice, sake, salt, and pepper. Mix well by hand until sticky. Add water and mix again. Add starch and sesame oil. Mix well.
2. Divide the filling up evenly and place in the center of wonton skins. Fold into triangles and fold in ends, making wontons into a hat shape.
3. Combine sauce ingredients. Cut bok choy lengthwise into bite-size clusters.
4. Bring water to a boil and add gyoza one at a time. Boil for three minutes then drain, reserving boiling liquid. Boil bok choy in the boiling liquid and arrange on a dish with gyoza in the center. Pour on sauce.

TIP: *Tianjiangyou* is soy sauce with a strong sweet flavor and thick consistency. You can make it at home. Fill a sauce pan with 2 1/2 C soy sauce, 8 3/4 oz (250 g) sugar, 1/2 C (125 ml) *Shaoxing* wine (or sake), 1 3/4 oz (50 g) thinly sliced ginger, 1/8 oz (4 g) each cinnamon stick, orange peel, Sichuan peppercorn (*hua jiao*), and star anise. Mix well until sugar dissolves and simmer at low heat for 1 to 1 1/2 hours, mixing occasionally. *Tianjiangyou* adds a robust flavor and a nice finish to sauces and simmered dishes.

It's important to mix the seasonings into the meat until it's sticky. This makes the filling soft and juicy.

Make gyoza. First, wet edges and fold up the bottom to make a triangle, but leave space at the top; don't line up the top corners perfectly.

Wet one of the lower corners with a little water. I use a small metal spatula, which comes in handy for adding the filling as well.

Attach moistened corner to the opposite side and press together firmly.

Now you have a cute little hat-shaped gyoza. Be careful not to add too much filling, or the shape won't come out right.

Combine sauce ingredients and mix well.

Boil water and drop in gyoza one by one in quick succession. Boil bok choy in the same water.

Boiling in plenty water helps prevent dumplings from sticking together.

"The spice makes the dish"—that's the motto of Sichuan cuisine. This dish uses 3 different kinds of spice: Doubanjiang, chili oil, and cayenne pepper. Adjust the amount to suit your taste.

Hot and Spicy Garlic Shrimp

Ingredients (serves 4)
8 whole jumbo shrimp
1/4 bunch rapini (broccoli raab)
Potato (or corn) starch
Oil for deep-frying
1/4 tomato
4" (10 cm) bunching onion
   (or green onion)
1 tsp garlic, minced
2 tsp ginger, minced
2 Tbsp vegetable oil
1/2 C soup stock
A ┌ 1 Tbsp Doubanjiang
      (Chinese chili paste)
  ├ 1 Tbsp chili oil
  └ 1 tsp cayenne pepper
B ┌ 1 Tbsp sake
  ├ 1 tsp sugar
  └ Dash each salt and pepper
Rice vinegar

1. Split open unshelled shrimp along the back and devein. Coat the back with starch.
2. Blanch rapini in boiling water briefly, coat in starch and deep-fry. Dice tomatoes and mince bunching onion.
3. Heat oil in a wok and add shrimp. Don't overlap. Stir-fry until crispy and remove from wok. Add diced tomato to wok and sauté. Add garlic and ginger and sauté slowly. Add mixture A and continue sautéing.
4. Add shrimp, soup stock and B ingredients and simmer. Add bunching onion and continue simmering until water evaporates and sauce thickens. Add fried rapini and finish with vinegar.

Stir-fry shrimp with the shells on. Cut the backs open and coat the openings with starch.

Use very ripe tomatoes.

Avoid overlapping when adding shrimp to wok.

Cook until shrimp shells are crispy and remove from wok.

Use the same wok to sauté tomato. Add garlic and ginger.

Sauté slowly and thoroughly to bring out the fragrant aroma of the garlic and ginger.

Add spicy seasonings and continue stir-frying to bring out the rich flavor of Doubanjiang. Add shrimp.

Pour in soup. Stir-fry well to bring out the flavors.

After adding bunching onion, simmer well until water evaporates and sauce thickens. Add rapini and vinegar to finish.

About Pre-seasoning

Chinese cuisine often calls for meat and seafood to be seasoned before cooking. Not only does this allow the seasonings to be absorbed well, it also serves to make meat soft and tender. Add seasonings and massage in well. Make sure they are well absorbed. Always use your hands, and take care to massage gently and thoroughly.

Fry the fish whole, simmer, and present it to the table.

Impressive, isn't it?

Spice-Simmered Fish

Ingredients (serves 4)
1 large black rockfish (*mebaru*)
  (or snapper or halibut)
2 tsp soy sauce
Oil, for deep-frying
4" (10 cm) bunching onion
2 Tbsp celery, minced
1 Tbsp vegetable oil
A ┌2 tsp grated ginger
  │ 1 tsp grated garlic
  │ 1 heaping Tbsp Doubanjiang
  └ (Chinese chili paste)
1 1/4 C soup stock
B ┌1 Tbsp sake
  │ 1 tsp sugar
  │ 2 tsp soy sauce
  └Dash each salt and pepper
2 to 3 Tbsp starch paste (see below)
1 Tbsp chili oil
1 Tbsp rice vinegar

1. Remove fish scales and innards. Score on the bias in 3 places on each side to facilitate cooking. Coat with 2 Tbsp soy sauce and let sit. Mince bunching onion.

2. Pat fish dry with a paper towel to remove juices and fry in oil heated to 390°F (200°C). Deep-fry without touching the fish until it's crispy on the outside.

3. Heat oil in a wok and sauté mixture A until fragrant. Add celery, soup stock, and mixture B. Stir briefly, add fried fish, and cover wok. Reduce heat to low and simmer, occasionally ladling sauce over fish. Continue simmering until liquid is reduced by half.

4. Add bunching onion and thicken sauce with starch paste. Rock wok to avoid burning. Finish with chili oil and rice vinegar. Turn off heat.

About Starch Paste

Adding starch paste makes it possible to turn cooking liquid into a thick sauce. This is a popular technique in Chinese cuisine. The paste is made with equal parts of water and potato or corn starch. If the recipe calls for 2 Tbsp of starch paste, use 1 Tbsp each of starch and water. Mix paste ahead of time for ease of use; however, the starch will precipitate, so stir well before use.

After gutting, make 2 to 3 diagonal cuts on each side. This is to ensure thorough cooking when frying.

Coat with soy sauce and let sit. Flip over and soak the other side for even flavor distribution.

Wiping juices from the fish before frying helps remove fishy smell.

Fry fish in very hot oil, sliding in gently to prevent oil from splashing out. Don't touch fish until crispy on the outside.

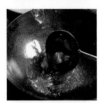

Add garlic, ginger and Doubanjiang. Stir-fry well until fragrant.

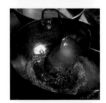

Add soup, sprinkle in celery, and add seasonings.

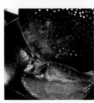

Add fried fish to wok, cover with a lid and simmer. Use low heat.

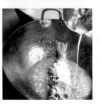

When sauce is reduced by half, add bunching onion and starch paste. Coat fish well with sauce.

You can tell this dish is spicy just by looking at it.
It's so spicy it'll make you sweat, even in winter.
Add roasted chilies and plenty of *hua jiao* for the finishing touch.
I recommend trying it on top of rice.

Simmered Beef with Vegetables

Ingredients (serves 4)

3 1/2 oz (100 g) lean beef, thinly sliced
A ⎡ 1/4 tsp salt
⎢ Dash pepper
⎢ 2 Tbsp sake (or cooking wine)
⎢ 1/2 egg
⎢ 2 Tbsp thick starch paste
⎣ 2 Tbsp starch
2 Napa cabbage leaves
2 scallions
1 Tbsp vegetable oil
2 Tbsp Doubanjiang (Chinese chili paste)
1 3/4 C soup stock
B ⎡ 1 Tbsp sake
⎢ 1 Tbsp soy sauce
⎣ Dash each sugar and pepper
C ⎡ Dash each roasted chili pepper,
⎢   Sichuan peppercorns (*hua jiao*),
⎣   red pepper oil

1. Place bite-size pieces of beef in a bowl and add 1st half of mixture A (from salt to sake). Mix well by hand. Add egg and starch paste and mix thoroughly. Massage in potato starch 1 Tbsp at a time.
2. Cut cabbage into large rectangular pieces. Cut scallions diagonally into 3/4" (2 cm) wide slices. Separate the white part from the green leaves.
3. Heat oil in a wok and sauté Doubanjiang gradually. Add soup and bring to a boil. Add cabbage and the white part of scallions to soup and boil until cabbage is slightly tender. Add mixture B and cook until cabbage is thoroughly soft. Transfer cabbage to a serving dish.
4. Use remaining soup to boil beef, adding each slice one by one. Add green leaves of scallions and mixture C. Transfer to dish, placing on top of cabbage.

TIP: Roasted chili peppers are good to have on hand if you like spicy food. Sauté 2 deseeded chili peppers in 3 Tbsp of oil. Remove, slice, and the chilies are ready. You can use the oil, too.

When seasoning beef, add the first 3 seasonings first, then coat with egg and starch paste.

Add potato starch 1 Tbsp at a time and massage in. This allows for absorption of flavor and also makes meat light and tender.

As always, sauté Doubanjiang thoroughly to bring out the full aroma.

Add soup stock and mix well before bringing to a boil.

Simmer cabbage thoroughly together with the white parts of scallions until the core of cabbage is tender.

Mix occasionally to cook evenly. Add soy sauce, sake and seasonings once vegetables become translucent, then simmer.

Transfer well-cooked cabbage to a dish. Remaining soup will be used to cook beef.

Add beef one slice at a time.

Stir beef to cook evenly.

Add the green leaves of scallions to beef and mix in briefly.

Finish with roasted chili pepper and *hua jiao* and serve on top of cabbage.

Crunchy Beef Sauté

Do you know the Japanese dish *kinpira*?
This is basically the super-spicy meat version of that dish.
You might want to breathe through your mouth when you make it,
or all the spices will make you sneeze.

Ingredients (serves 4)
3 1/2 oz (100 g) beef thigh, thinly
   sliced
2 3/4 oz (80 g) celery
2 3/4 oz (80 g) carrot
4" (10 cm) bunching onion
   (or green onion)
2 red chili peppers, deseeded
20 grains Sichuan peppercorn
   (*hua jiao*)
2 Tbsp vegetable oil
2 tsp Doubanjiang
   (Chinese chili paste)
2 tsp sweet noodle sauce
   (*tianmianjiang*. Or Hoisin sauce)
A ┌1/2 tsp sugar
   │ 1 Tbsp each soy sauce and sake
   └Dash pepper
Dash each rice vinegar and ground
   Sichuan pepper (*hua jiao fen*)

1. Cut beef into thin strips. Cut celery and carrot into 2" (5 to 6 cm) long strips. Slice red chili peppers into rounds.
2. Heat oil in a wok and sauté Sichuan peppercorns and chili peppers. Remove once oil becomes fragrant and spicy. Add beef to wok and sauté until crispy. Add Doubanjiang and soy sauce and stir-fry well.
3. Add vegetables and stir-fry until tender. Add mixture A, stir-fry briskly at high heat, and add minced bunching onion. Mix together and finish with rice vinegar. Transfer to a dish and sprinkle with ground Sichuan pepper.

Spice the oil first by sautéing chilies and peppercorn, then remove. If you leave them in they will burn and turn bitter.

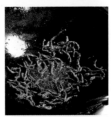

Take your time and cook beef well until it's nicely browned.

Cook celery and carrot just until tender, then add seasonings.

5

Intercultural Treats from My Mother's Kitchen

My father and I both loved my mother's creative combination of Chinese and Japanese cooking.

I should admit that when I was a kid I sometimes complained about my mother's cooking because she'd make a big pot full of one dish and feed us the same thing for days on end.

Simmered Daikon with Shrimp

Ingredients (serves 4 to 5)
1 daikon radish, peeled
1 3/4 oz (50 g) fresh *sakura* shrimp
 (dwarf shrimp)
2 Tbsp vegetable oil
2 Tbsp Doubanjiang
4 C soup stock
1 Tbsp sugar
2 Tbsp sake
1 Tbsp soy sauce
Snow peas

1. Cut daikon into 2" (5 cm) thick half-moon slices and boil until translucent.
2. Heat oil in a wok and sauté Doubanjiang. Add daikon and pour in soup stock. Add *sakura* shrimp, sugar, and sake. Bring to a boil and remove bitter foam that floats to the top. Reduce heat to a low boil and simmer for approximately 40 min. Add soy sauce to adjust flavor.
3. Transfer to a dish and add oil and salt to finish. Garnish with boiled snow peas cut into bite-size pieces.

TIP: This dish is even better if you let it sit for a while so that the daikon slices can absorb the flavor thoroughly.

Add *sakura* shrimp to boiled daikon and simmer in soup. The shrimp flavor the soup so best to add them early on.

Scoop out the foam resulting from simmering daikon and shrimp.

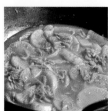

Simmer for approximately 40 minutes after boiling to make daikon delectably tender and allow flavor to blend into the soup.

Stir-fry of Pickled Daikon and *Kamaboko*

My father was a big fan of pickled daikon, and he had a habit of buying *kamaboko* as a souvenir whenever he went on a trip. I figure that's what gave my mother the idea for this dish. Try it on plain rice, or mixed in with fried rice.

Ingredients (serves 4 to 6)
7 oz (200g) sweet pickled daikon
  (*takuan*)
1 fish sausage (*kamaboko*)
1 bundle spring onions
  (or scallions)
1 Tbsp sesame oil
2 tsp sugar
1 tsp soy sauce
5 Tbsp roasted white sesame seeds

1. Cut pickled daikon into 3 1/4"
(7 to 8 cm) pieces, then julienne.
Cut fish sausage in half, then into
1/8" (3 mm) thick slices, then julienne.
2. Heat sesame oil in a wok and
stir-fry pickled daikon well until
moisture has evaporated. Add fish
sausage and stir-fry quickly. Season
with sugar and soy sauce and
quickly mix in spring onions. Sprinkle
with sesame seeds and turn off
heat.

TIP: The key is to stir-fry pickled
daikon thoroughly until it becomes
lightly charred. And be generous
with the sesame seeds.

Stir-fry pickled
daikon thoroughly
in sesame oil until
crunchy.

Pressed Tofu with Chrysanthemum

This elegant dish is geared for grown-ups. I was able to enjoy it as a kid because my mother cooked the chrysanthemum until very tender and chopped it finely. Don't add too much salt because the shrimp is salty, too.

Ingredients (serves 4)
1 bundle edible chrysanthemum
  (*shungiku*. Or sub. spinach)
1 block pressed tofu
1 oz (30 g) dried shrimp,
  reconstituted
Dash each sugar, salt and soy sauce
1 1/2 Tbsp sesame oil

1. Boil chrysanthemum until tender. "Shock" in ice water to cool, then drain. Squeeze to remove excess water and chop into very fine pieces to break up the fibers.
2. Boil pressed tofu and dice into small 1/8" (3 mm) cubes. Mince reconstituted shrimp.
3. Combine chrysanthemum, tofu and shrimp in a bowl and season with sugar, salt, soy sauce, and sesame oil. Mix well.

Squeeze out water from bright green boiled chrysanthemum and chop finely. The finer it's chopped, the tastier it gets.

Cut pressed tofu into small pieces and mince shrimp. Mix all ingredients well for even distribution.

Pressed tofu is made by wrapping firm tofu in cheesecloth and pressing it under a weight. It's easy to make at home. Just boil firm tofu in salted water, wrap in cheesecloth and press.

This was my favorite meal growing up.

If my mother said, "Steak for dinner tonight!" my head would be filled

with mouth-watering visions all day at school.

I headed straight home on those days.

However, my mother didn't dress the plate with watercress like I do here.

Chinese-Style Steak

Ingredients (serves 1)
1 cut beef tenderloin
Dash each salt and pepper
1 onion
Beef tallow or vegetable oil
A ┌ Dash soy sauce
  │ 1 Tbsp sake
  └ 1 tsp soy sauce
Watercress, for garnish

1.   Score meat diagonally along the surface of the beef and season with salt and pepper. Thinly slice onion against the grain.
2.   Melt beef tallow in a wok and add steak. Grill on both sides to desired level of doneness and remove from wok. Use remaining fat in pan to sauté onions. Add mixture A.
3.   Cut steak into bite-size strips, top with sautéed onions and garnish plate with watercress.

TIP: I like Worcestershire sauce with my steak, but you can substitute soy sauce according to your preference. The shallow scoring makes the meat tender, so this recipe works well even with inexpensive cuts of meat.

If you score the meat like this, you can enjoy your steak without using a knife, and even cheaper cuts come out delicious.

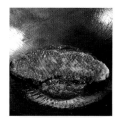

The steak is served sliced, but consider which side you will serve facing up and cook that side first. Cook rare, medium-well—however you like it.

Place the grilled steak on top of pre-arranged chopsticks or skewers to allow excess oil to drip off and the flavor to seep in.

Use leftover tallow or oil from grilling steak to sauté the onions.

Sauté onions until translucent and tender, then season. The juices from the steak add a delicious flavor.

The sound of a sizzling wok, the scrape of a metal ladle as it moves quickly across the surface—then flip—and the rice flies through the air in a graceful arc. I've been making my own fried rice since middle school. I wanted to learn how because I thought it looked so cool. The key to delicious fried rice is a well-heated and well-oiled wok.

Chen-Style Fried Rice

Ingredients (serves 2)
21 oz (600 g) cooked rice
2 3/4 oz (80 g) wiener (hot dog)
1 3/4 oz (50 g) carrot
1/2 cucumber
1 3/4 oz (50 g) onion
3 to 4 Tbsp vegetable oil
1/4 tsp salt
Dash pepper
2 tsp soy sauce

1. Mince wiener. Peel carrot and cucumber and remove seeds from cucumber. Mince carrot, cucumber, and onion.
2. Heat 2 Tbsp oil in a wok and add minced wiener. Fry until crispy and aromatic. Add minced vegetables and stir-fry. Add remaining oil and add rice to wok. Stir-fry, mixing rice into other ingredients.
3. Continue to stir-fry until well blended, then season with salt and pepper. Pour soy sauce in a circular motion directly onto the surface of wok and mix in quickly.

Stir-fry minced wiener well until crispy and aromatic.

Add minced vegetables and stir-fry. Vegetables should be about the same size as the minced wiener.

Stir-fry quickly at high heat until vegetables are tender.

Add rice. If clumps form, break up as you stir.

Stir-fry quickly, scooping up from the bottom and turning over to mix well. Use high heat.

Stir in salt and pepper. Add soy sauce at the end to take best advantage of its full aroma.

Fried Rice with Pickles and Young Sardines

Ingredients (serves 2)
21 oz (600 g) cooked rice
3/4 oz (20 g) pickled turnip stems (*nozawana*)
3/4 oz (20 g) small pickled plums (*umezuke*)
3/4 oz (20 g) baby sardines (*jako*)
4" (10 cm) bunching onion (or green onion)
2 eggs
3 Tbsp vegetable oil
1 tsp salt
Dash pepper

1. Mince pickled turnip stems, pickled plums and bunching onion. Lightly beat egg just enough to combine white and yolk.
2. Coat heated wok thoroughly with oil. Pour in egg all at once. Stir-fry at high heat. When egg is half-cooked, add rice and stir-fry, blending well.
3. Add minced turnip stems and sardines. Flip rice out of the wok or scoop from the bottom and turn over with a spatula or ladle. Season with salt and pepper. Add bunching onion and stir-fry at high heat.

To stir-fry an egg you need a wok so well-oiled it's shiny. Pour in egg all at once.

Allow egg to cook undisturbed until edges bubble. Then, stir quickly with large movements two or three times.

Add rice while egg is still half-cooked. Act quickly or the egg will over-cook.

Mix egg and rice by flipping the wok or by scooping from the bottom with a ladle or spatula.

I suggest cooking fried rice one serving at a time. That's how the pros do it. If you can't gracefully flip the rice out of the wok, don't worry about it. Better to use a spatula and avoid having it end up all over the floor.

Stir-fry quickly to mix egg evenly through-out the rice.

Combining ingredients be-forehand makes it easier to add while cooking.

Season with salt and pepper. Add bunching onion at the end.

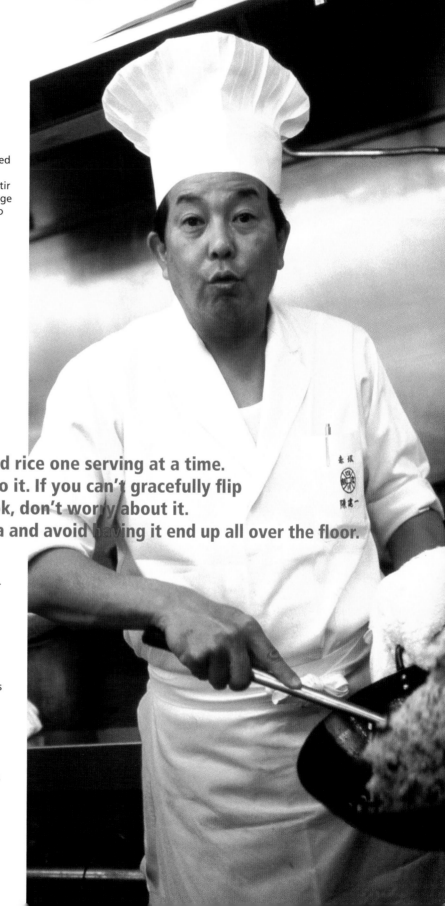

Egg Fried Rice with Cream Sauce

Ingredients (serves 2)
21 oz (600 g) cooked rice
2 eggs
4" (10 cm) bunching onion
   (or green onion)
3 Tbsp vegetable oil
1/2 tsp salt
Dash pepper
Cream Sauce:
   8 shelled shrimp
   2 3/4 oz (50 g) boiled crabmeat
   1 leaf Napa cabbage
   3 baby corn, canned
   3/4 oz (20 g) edamame (green
      soybeans), boiled and peeled
   2 Tbsp vegetable oil
   1 1/4 C soup stock
   1 Tbsp sake
   1/3 tsp salt
   Dash each sugar and pepper
   3 Tbsp starch paste
      (see Reference Guide)
   3 Tbsp evaporated milk

Start with the shrimp. Quickly fry in the wok.

Half-cooked eggs are best for fried rice.

Once shrimp changes color, set aside, then add Napa cabbage and baby corn, and stir-fry.

After adding rice, flip wok or turn over mixture by scooping up from bottom with a ladle.

Add crabmeat and edamame once Napa cabbage is tender.

Mix the egg into the rice thoroughly.

Add evaporated milk to give the sauce a rich, creamy flavor.

Add salt, pepper and bunching onion, and stir-fry briefly. Serve on a dish and top with cream sauce.

Fried rice, egg, cream sauce, shrimp and Napa cabbage. This well-balanced combination of mellow flavors is great when you want a break from the usual tongue-numbing Sichuan fare.

1. Make cream sauce. Devein shrimp. Divide Napa cabbage into leaves and stems and cut into large bite-size pieces. Cut baby corn into halves.

2. Heat oil in wok and add shrimp. Fry just until color changes and remove from wok. Add stems of Napa cabbage to wok, then add baby corn and cabbage leaves in that order. Stir-fry and add soup stock. Bring to a boil and simmer.

3. When cabbage is tender add crabmeat, edamame, sake, salt, sugar and pepper. Return shrimp to wok and thicken sauce with starch paste. Add evaporated milk to finish sauce.

4. Make fried rice. Lightly beat egg just enough to combine white and yolk. Mince bunching onion. Heat oil in a new wok and add egg all at once. Stir quickly. When eggs are half-done add rice. Mix thoroughly, making sure rice doesn't clump.

5. Season rice with salt and pepper and sprinkle in minced bunching onion. Stir-fry. Transfer to a dish and top with cream sauce.

TIP: It's best to use warm rice when making fried rice. If using cold rice try sprinkling on a bit of sake and breaking up any clumps before adding to the wok.

Chicken and Egg Soup

Put your food processor to good use in making this light-as-air chicken and egg white soup. It's important to cook slowly and carefully until soup turns clear.

Ingredients (serves 4)
7 oz (200 g) chicken breast
4 egg whites
1 1/4 cold soup stock
A ┌ 1/3 tsp salt
  │ 1 Tbsp sake
  │ 2 Tbsp starch paste
  └ (see Reference Guide)
B ┌ 4 C soup stock
  │ 1 Tbsp sake
  │ 1/2 tsp salt
  └ Dash pepper
Chives, to taste

1. Chop up chicken breast and place in a food processor together with egg whites and soup stock. Process until liquidized. Transfer to a bowl and add mixture A.

2. Place mixture B in a wok and bring to a boil. Lower heat and gently pour in chicken soup one ladleful at a time. Wait until chicken becomes cooked and floats to the surface before adding successive spoonfuls. Remove surface foam.

3. When all of chicken mixture has been added, simmer for 5 to 6 minutes, occasionally stirring slowly. When soup turns clear, turn off heat and transfer to dishes. Sprinkle with chopped chives.

TIP: Getting the heat level right is essential. Keep the soup at a low, gently bubbling boil or it will become cloudy.

Chop chicken first before adding to food processor. Add egg white and soup stock.

Mix in the food processor until thick and creamy. Transfer to a bowl.

Season with salt and sake. Add starch paste.

Bring mixture B to a boil. Add chicken mixture slowly.

Cook soup at low heat until soup turns clear, stirring occasionally. Stir slowly and gently.

Transfer soup to a bowl, garnish with chives, and serve.

See Reference Guide for how to prepare soup stock.

Steamed Cabbage Soup

Chicken drumstick, dried scallop and bacon are all great ingredients for making soup stock. No wonder this steamed soup is so delicious. This is a secret technique for delicious homemade soups.

Ingredients (serves 4)
1/4 cabbage
1 chicken drumstick (with bone)
4 slices bacon
2 dried scallops (reconstituted)
1 bunching onion
   (or green onion)
1 nub ginger
4 C soup stock
A ⌈4 Tbsp sake
  │ 1/2 tsp salt
  └Dash pepper

1. Core cabbage and cut in half lengthwise. Cut bacon into 2" (5 to 6 cm) pieces. Shred dried scallops and cut bunching onion diagonally into large pieces. Cut ginger into decorative shapes or thin slices.

2. Bring water to a boil in wok and add chicken and cabbage. When cabbage is tender remove and rinse in water to cool. Transfer to a colander and drain. Boil chicken for 5 to 6 minutes, removing foam that floats to the surface, then remove chicken from wok.

3. Place boiled cabbage and chicken in a stainless steel bowl. Add bacon, scallops, bunching onion, and ginger. Pour in soup stock and mixture A and cover bowl with aluminum foil. Place bowl in a steamer and steam for approximately one hour until cabbage is completely tender.

TIP: The chicken thigh is mainly used just for the broth, but you can shred the meat from the bone and enjoy it in the soup or separately as a dressed dish.

Heat water to a rolling boil and add chicken and cabbage.

Boil cabbage until tender, then cool in water. Drain. Cook chicken for 5 to 6 minutes longer.

Place cabbage and chicken in a bowl. Spread bacon out on top.

Place shredded scallop, bunching onion and ginger on top of the bacon slices.

Pour in soup stock and seasonings, cover with foil and steam. Make sure that the foil is on tightly, like a lid.

About Bamboo Steamers

For steaming, I suggest using a bamboo steamer. It has a curved wooden frame with a base of woven bamboo. Place it on top of a wok filled with boiling water. It's convenient because you can stack several tiers one on top of another. The woven bamboo lets just enough steam through without making the contents too soggy, and it's easy to add more water to the wok underneath. You can use an ordinary steamer too, of course, but be careful to add enough water at the beginning if you do.

**Steam the bowl after covering securely with aluminum foil.
I know it's tempting to take a peek and see how the soup is doing.
But don't give in! Leaving the lid on is important for this dish
to come out delicious.**

Steamed Pork Soup

Ingredients (serves 4)

7 oz (200 g) pork loin, thinly
   sliced
1 3/4 oz (50 g) Napa cabbage
1 dried shiitake mushroom
   (reconstituted)
1 dried scallop (reconstituted)
3/4 oz (20 g) Chinese ham
   (or Smithfield ham)
1 3/4 oz (50 g) boiled bamboo
   shoots
A ┌ 2 Tbsp sake
  │ 1 Tbsp soy sauce
  │ 1/3 tsp salt
  └ Dash pepper

1. Score pork and chop finely.
Mince Napa cabbage and
shiitake with stems removed.
Shred scallops and mince Chinese ham and boiled bamboo
shoots.
2. Place minced pork in a
bowl and add 1 C of water
1/4 C at a time, stirring by
hand each time. Add remaining ingredients and mix well.
Add mixture A.
3. Divide soup mixture into
individual cups and cover
tightly with aluminum foil.
Place in a heated steamer
and steam at high heat for
approximately 1 hour.

TIP: Watching the water level
is easy if you use a bamboo
steamer. If using a regular
steamer be careful not to let
it run out of water.

Score pork, then
chop finely.

The Napa cabbage
and other ingredients
should be minced to
approximately same
size as the pork.

Add pork to a bowl,
mix with 1/4 C water,
and stir well by hand
until sticky.

When the pork has
thoroughly absorbed
water, add 1/4 C
more and stir by
hand again. Repeat
this process until 1
C of water is mixed
into the pork.

Add remaining
ingredients to pork
mixture.

Again, mix well
by hand.

Add seasonings and mix
in well. Divide
mixture up
into individual
dishes.

Cover tightly
with foil and
steam. Don't
remove foil
until done.

7

Refreshing Fruit Dishes

Enjoy the first-time experience of these surprisingly delectable dishes.

This recipe is my father's original creation.

In the Sichuan province, spinach was used instead of Muscat grapes.

The subtle flavor of dad's grape version is a good way to

refresh your taste buds.

Muscat Grapes with Chicken

Ingredients (serves 4)

12 large muscat grapes
Potato (or corn) starch

Coating:
- 2 3/4 oz (80 g) chicken breast
- 1 Tbsp sake
- 1 Tbsp evaporated milk
- 2 tsp soup stock
- Dash each salt, pepper and sugar
- 2 egg whites
- 1 tsp potato (or corn) starch

Sauce:
- 1 C soup stock
- 1 Tbsp sake
- Dash salt
- 2 Tbsp starch paste (see Reference Guide)

Spring onions (or scallions), chopped

1. Remove skins of muscat grapes by blanching in boiling water, then cool by placing in ice water. Remove seeds using a fine skewer.
2. Make coating. Mince chicken breast finely and place in a bowl. Add sake, evaporated milk and soup. Mix thoroughly by hand until it turns into a paste.
3. Season chicken paste with salt, pepper and sugar and knead well. Beat egg whites until they form stiff peaks, then add to chicken paste. Add starch and mix in quickly.
4. Coat grapes with starch. Pierce one at a time with a fine skewer and coat with chicken paste. Drop into boiling water and cook. Drain coated grapes, cut in half and arrange on a dish.
5. Place all sauce ingredients except starch paste in a wok and bring to a boil. Thicken with starch paste and pour over grapes. Sprinkle on chopped spring onions.

TIP: When boiling coated grapes, use gently bubbling boiling water.

Thoroughly mince chicken and then add other ingredients in listed order. Mix thoroughly by hand, gently but with some force.

Once you add the sugar, you should have a smooth paste, like this.

Beat egg whites into stiff peaks as if making a meringue. Stir in gently with hands and be careful not to ruin the foamy texture.

Using a bamboo skewer is the best way to coat grapes. Dip skewered grapes in coating, twirl around and drop into boiling water.

Keep water at a gentle boil. When grapes float up to the surface, they are ready.

Drain coated grapes well. Otherwise, they're too soggy.

Carefully pour sauce over halved grapes arranged on a plate and serve.

Candied sweet potatoes is a popular dish in Japan.
This is a banana verison of that dish.
Simmer honey and water until golden and add fried bananas,
stirring until thoroughly coated.

Honey-Coated Fried Bananas

Ingredients (serves 4)
2 bananas
Potato (or corn) starch
Batter:
- 1 1/2 oz (40 g) flour
- 1/2 oz (15 g) potato starch
- 1/2 egg
- 2 Tbsp water
- 1 egg white

Oil for deep-frying
2 Tbsp water
2 Tbsp honey
Roasted sesame seeds

1. Cut banana into 1/2 to 1" (1.5 to 2 cm) rounds and coat thoroughly with starch.
2. Combine all batter ingredients except for egg white and mix well. Beat egg white until stiff peaks form, then add to batter mixture. Dip banana rounds in batter and fry in 250 to 265°F (120 to 130°C) oil until coating becomes crispy.
3. Empty wok of oil and add water and honey. Simmer on low heat, stirring constantly, until it turns a deep golden color. Add fried bananas to wok and stir in with large sweeping motions to coat thoroughly. Sprinkle on sesame seeds before serving.

Coat banana with starch thoroughly so the batter will stick.

Coat banana with batter. Best to use your hands here.

Add bananas one by one to relatively cool frying oil.

When bananas turn a light, crispy golden brown, they're ready.

When simmering honey use low heat and stir constantly. It will slowly turn a beautiful golden color.

Add fried bananas and stir, swishing across the wok with large sweeping motions to coat thoroughly.

The batter here is the same as for the previous banana recipe.

Hold cherry by the stem, dip in batter and fry until crispy. That's it.

Don't overcook or the cherries will get mushy.

Stir-fried Shrimp with Cherries

Ingredients (serves 4)
12 cherries
Potato (or corn) starch
Batter:
   1 1/2 oz (40 g) flour
   1/2 oz (15 g) potato (or corn) starch
   1/2 egg
   2 Tbsp water
   1 egg white
Oil for deep-frying
5 1/4 oz (150 g) shelled shrimp
A Dash each salt and pepper
   White of 1 large egg
   1 heaping Tbsp potato starch
2 red chili peppers
4" (10 cm) bunching onion (or green onion)
1 tsp ginger, grated
1 Tbsp vegetable oil
B 1 Tbsp sake
   1 Tbsp rice vinegar
   1 Tbsp soup stock
   1 1/3 Tbsp sugar
   1 1/2 Tbsp soy sauce
   Dash pepper
   1 Tbsp starch paste (see Reference Guide)

1. Cut deseeded chili peppers into 1/3" (1 cm) slices and bunching onion into 1/6" (5 mm) diagonal slices. Devein shrimp and season with mixture A.

2. Follow instructions on page 75 to make batter. Coat cherries with starch, dip in batter, and fry at low heat (250°F (120°C)). Drain oil.

3. Raise oil to a temperature of 320 to 340°F (160 to 170°C) and dip shrimp into hot oil briefly. Empty wok of oil.

4. Add vegetable oil to wok and stir-fry chili peppers slowly at low heat until charred. Add bunching onion and ginger and stir-fry well at low heat until fragrant. Add fried shrimp and cherries. Combine mixture B, mix, then pour into wok, and stir-fry quickly at high heat.

Coat cherries thoroughly with starch, being careful not to remove stems.

Dip cherries in batter one by one, holding by stems.

Drop gently into frying oil. Use very low heat, no more than 250°F (120°C).

Fry just until coating becomes lightly crispy and remove immediately from oil. Over-frying will make cherries mushy.

Shrimp should be dipped in oil briefly. Be careful not to overcook.

Keep heat at low and sauté chili peppers slowly until blackened. Add bunching onion and ginger and sauté until fragrant.

Return cherries and shrimp to wok, season with mixture B and stir-fry. Use high heat.

Use large sweeping ladle movements to stir so as not to crush cherries.

It's the lightweight crust that makes this dish fantastic. To cook thoroughly, start at low heat and slowly raise the temperature until the outer crust is golden and crispy.

Pork and Apple Fritters

Ingredients (serves 4)

1 apple

Potato (or corn) starch

3 1/2 oz (100 g) ground pork

A ┌ Dash salt
   │ 1 Tbsp sake
   │ 1 tsp ginger, grated
   │ 1 egg, lightly beaten
   │ 1 tsp sesame oil
   └ 1 tsp potato starch

Batter:

┌ 1 egg
│ 1/4 C water
│ 3 1/2 oz (100 g) flour
│ 1 3/4 oz (50 g) potato starch
│ 1 Tbsp baking powder
│ Dash salt
└ 1 Tbsp vegetable oil

Oil for deep-frying

Sauce:

┌ 2 Tbsp vegetable oil
│ 1 tsp garlic, grated
│ 2 tsp ginger, grated
│ 1 Tbsp Doubanjiang (Chinese chili paste)
│ 1 C soup stock
│ 1 Tbsp sake
│ 1 Tbsp sugar
│ 2 tsp soy sauce
│ Dash pepper
│ 2" (5 cm) bunching onion, minced
│ 2 Tbsp starch paste (see Reference Guide)
└ 1/2 Tbsp rice vinegar

1. Core and quarter apple, then slice into approximately 20 half-moon slices.

2. Add mixture A ingredients to pork in listed order and mix well. Divide into 10 equal parts and sandwich each portion between two slices of apple.

3. Mix batter ingredients and coat apple and pork sandwiches one by one. Fry in oil, raising the temperature gradually, until crust is crispy. Drain oil and cut into bite-size pieces. Arrange on a dish.

4. Make sauce. Empty frying wok of oil and heat vegetable oil. Add grated garlic, ginger and Doubanjiang and sauté well. Add to this all remaining ingredients except for starch paste and rice vinegar and bring to a boil. Thicken sauce with starch paste, add vinegar, and turn off heat. Pour over fritters.

Sandwich seasoned pork like this between two apple slices. If you blend pork thoroughly, the apple slices will stick.

Keep pork filling at a uniform thickness to ensure even cooking. This recipe makes 10 fritters.

Add batter ingredients in order and use your hands like a blender to mix in a circular motion.

Finish by adding vegetable oil for a smooth and creamy batter.

Start with 280 to 300°F oil and slowly raise the temperature. Otherwise, the coating will burn before the apples are cooked.

Gradually raise the temperature and fry until golden and crispy. Be sure to drain oil well.

Sauté garlic, ginger and Doubanjiang at low heat first to bring out fragrance. Then add soup stock, sake and other ingredients.

8

Scrumptious Seasonal Stir-fries

Unleash the incomparable flavor of freshly harvested vegetables with these seasonal recipes.

S
P
R
I
N
G

Stir-fried Chicken with Green Asparagus

The key to making the chicken tender is the order of seasoning: salt, sake, egg white and then starch. Massage in by hand and add oil.

Stir-fried Shrimp with Green Peas

Heat the wok and coat with oil. That's the secret to making a delicious stir-fry. Add seasonings, turn the heat up high, stir quickly and finish with sauce. Looks delicious, doesn't it?

Stir-fried Chicken with Green Asparagus

Ingredients (serves 4)

8 green asparagus
7 oz (200 g) skinless chicken breast
A ┌ 1/2 tsp salt
  │ 1 Tbsp sake
  │ White of 1 egg
  │ 1 heaping Tbsp potato starch
  └ 1 Tbsp vegetable oil
Oil for deep-frying
2" (5 cm) bunching onion
  (or green onion)
1 nub ginger
2 Tbsp vegetable oil
B ┌ 4 Tbsp soup stock
  │ 4 Tbsp evaporated milk
  │ 1/2 tsp sugar
  │ 1/3 tsp salt
  │ 1 Tbsp sake
  └ Dash pepper
2 Tbsp starch paste
  (see Reference Guide)

1.   Cut off root ends of asparagus and lightly peel skins. Cut in half and thinly slice lower half and quarter upper half. Thinly slice chicken then finely chop along the grain.

2.   Season chicken with mixture A, adding in listed order. Add chicken all at once to frying oil heated to 212°F (100°C). Separate to keep from clumping. Once chicken changes color, add asparagus then scoop out with a sieved ladle immediately, blanching in the oil. Remove chicken and empty wok of oil.

3.   Mince bunching onion and ginger. Heat 1 Tbsp vegetable oil in the wok and stir-fry onion and ginger. Add chicken and asparagus, pour in mixture B and stir-fry quickly. Finish with last 1 Tbsp oil.

TIP: When frying chicken in oil, keep the temperature low. If oil is too hot, the chicken will clump.

Cut off the root end of asparagus and peel the skin to ensure tenderness.

Use chopsticks to separate chicken while frying.

Cut asparagus in half and slice into equal parts for even cooking.

Dip the asparagus in oil briefly. Drain excess oil from wok.

Chop chicken and gently massage in seasoning ingredients in listed order. Done properly, this pre-seasoning ensures the meat will come out tender and juicy.

Stir-frying is easy when you use the same wok used for deep frying, since it's well-greased.

Keep heat low when cooking chicken in oil to prevent clumping.

Turn heat to high and stir-fry quickly after adding chicken and asparagus. Add sauce.

Stir-fried Shrimp with Green Peas

Ingredients (serves 4)

7 oz (200 g) shelled shrimp

A ⌈ Dash each salt pepper
  │ White of 1 large egg
  └ 1 heaping Tbsp potato starch

3 1/2 oz (100 g) green peas

2 Tbsp vegetable oil

4" (10 cm) bunching onion
   (or green onion)

1 nub ginger

B ⌈ 1 Tbsp sake
  │ 1/3 tsp salt
  │ 1/2 tsp sugar
  │ Dash pepper
  │ 1 tsp evaporated milk
  │ 1 Tbsp starch paste
  │   (see Reference Guide)
  └ 2 Tbsp soup stock

1. Devein shrimp and season with mixture A. Briefly boil green peas, leaving firm texture. Cut bunching onion diagonally into 2/5" (1 cm) pieces. Julienne ginger. Combine mixture B and stir well.

2. Heat oil in a wok and arrange shrimp along surface of wok. Sauté shrimp, flipping occasionally. Add bunching onion and ginger, stir-fry, add green peas and continue stir-frying. Pour in mixture B and finish quickly at high heat.

Sauté shrimp just until the outside is done. Poke the shrimp, and if the surface is tender, they're ready.

Add bunching onion, then ginger, then green peas.

Rock the wok to flip ingredients, and constantly stir with a ladle.

You can add the seasonings in the listed order, but it's easier to mix everything together ahead of time.

Using a Wok: About Greasing

A well-greased wok is essential for making a successful stir-fry dish. First, heat an empty wok over high heat until smoking-hot. Add a generous amount of oil to the hot wok. Swish oil around to coat the entire surface, then drain off excess oil. You can tell a well-greased wok by its shiny surface. Heat the wok again, and add vegetable oil for cooking. Stir-fry ingredients quickly at high heat.

Blanching and Draining

Blanching ingredients by dipping briefly in low-temperature frying oil is a technique used in Chinese cuisine. The temperature varies depending on what ingredients you use, as well as on size and amount, but the usual range is from 212 to 300°F (100 to 150°C). Vegetables are cooked quickly at a high temperature of around 350°F (180°C) and ingredients dipped in batter are cooked slowly at lower temperature to avoid burning. Fried vegetables can be rinsed of excess oil by pouring boiling water over them.

Stir-fried Bell Peppers

This colorful dish livens up the table. You can make this ahead of time and serve it chilled as an appetizer. Remember to soak *douchi* in water to tenderize.

Stir-fried *Kabocha*

Cook ground pork at high heat in plenty of oil to get it nice and crumbly. You can use any kind of Asian pickle in place of *zha cai*.

Tomato and Egg Stir-fry

The key here is cooking quickly in a well-greased wok over high heat, with sesame oil to finish. Sesame oil is the best oil for evaporating water, and it really enhances the flavor of the egg.

Stir-fried Bell Peppers

Ingredients (serves 4)

12 1/4 oz (350 g) giant bell peppers
    (1 each of red, green, orange and
    purple)
2 red chili peppers
1 Tbsp garlic, minced
2 Tbsp vegetable oil
A ⌐ 3/4 oz (20 g) fermented black
      beans (*douchi*), soaked in water
   1 tsp Doubanjiang
     (Chinese chili paste)
   └ 1 Tbsp sake
B ⌐ 2 tsp soy sauce
   Dash pepper
   └ 1 tsp each sesame oil and chili oil

1. Deseed bell peppers and chop into bite-size pieces. Deseed chili peppers and slice into rounds. Rinse minced garlic and drain to mellow out flavor.

2. Heat oil in a wok, add bell peppers and stir-fry slowly until tender and lightly browned.

3. Add chili peppers, garlic, and mixture A. Stir-fry, allowing water to evaporate, until fragrant. Add mixture B and stir-fry. Finish with sesame and chili oils.

TIP: When stir-frying, make sure there is enough oil to coat all the ingredients. It's okay to add more if there's not enough.

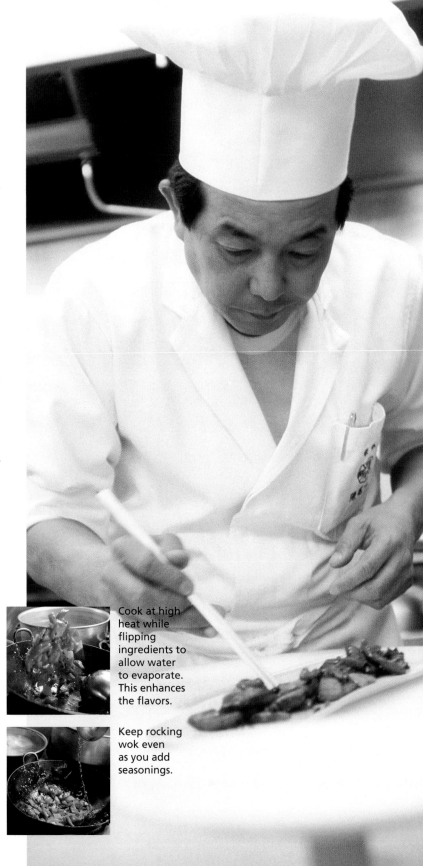

After removing seeds, cut bell peppers into pieces of similar size to ensure even cooking.

Cut all ingredients ahead of time. This kind of preparation is important when stir-frying. Keep seasoning ingredients within easy reach, too.

Cook at high heat while flipping ingredients to allow water to evaporate. This enhances the flavors.

Keep rocking wok even as you add seasonings.

Stir-fried *Kabocha*

Ingredients (serves 4)
300 g (10 1/2 oz) *kabocha*
  (aka Japanese pumpkin)
2 bunches spinach
3 1/2 oz (100 g) ground pork
3/4 oz (20 g) dried shrimp
3/4 oz (20 g) *zha cai*
  (Sichuan vegetable)
4" (10 cm) bunching onion
  (or green onion)
Oil, for deep-frying
2 Tbsp vegetable oil
A ⌐1 Tbsp sake
  │ Dash each salt and cayenne
  └   pepper
1 tsp each soy sauce and sesame oil

1. Dice *kabocha* into 2/5" (1 cm) cubes. Remove spinach roots and chop stems into 2/5" (1 cm) pieces, then mince leaves.
2. Rinse dried shrimp and soak in water for 20 to 30 minutes to reconstitute. Mince shrimp, *zha cai* and bunching onion.
3. Heat oil for frying in a wok and add *kabocha* all at once. Fry until cooked through and remove.
4. Drain wok and add oil for stir-frying. Sauté ground pork over high heat, add shrimp and *zha cai* and stir-fry. Return *kabocha* to wok, season with mixture A, and stir-fry. Add spinach. Flavor with soy sauce and sesame oil. Add bunching onion and stir-fry briefly.

To ensure even cooking, cut *kabocha* into identical pieces and vary cutting method for stems and leaves of spinach.

Stir and pour oil over *kabocha* constantly while cooking. Use high heat.

Fry *kabocha* until thoroughly cooked. It will be mixed in with other ingredients at the end.

Stir-fry pork and *zha cai* and return *kabocha* to wok.

Finish with minced bunching onion.

Tomato and Egg Stir-fry

Ingredients (serves 4)
1 tomato
4 eggs
5 spring onions (or scallions)
1 nub ginger
A ⌐2 Tbsp sake
  │ 1/3 tsp salt
  └Dash pepper
1 Tbsp starch paste
  (see Reference Guide)
3 Tbsp vegetable oil
Sesame oil, to taste

1. Blanch tomato in boiling water and peel skin. Slice into 8 equal segments, and cut each of these in half diagonally. Julienne ginger.
2. Blend yolk and egg white together, add mixture A and beat lightly, being careful not to incorporate air bubbles. Add starch paste and 1 tsp of sesame oil and mix. Add tomato, chives and ginger.
3. Heat vegetable oil in a wok and add egg mixture. Fry quickly over high heat, using a ladle to scoop and stir eggs. Finish with a sprinkle of sesame oil.

TIP: Slice ginger as thinly as possible, or it will overpower the mellow flavor of the egg.

Combine white and yolk in a bowl and season.
Stir gently—don't create bubbles.

Add other ingredients and stir quickly.

From here on speed is important. Use a well-greased wok and add egg all at once.

Keep the wok and ladle moving. Use large movements and high heat. If you take too much time, the tomatoes will "weep."

Add sesame oil for a finishing touch.

AUTUMN

Stir-fried Tofu with Mushrooms

Spicy seasoning goes well with the subtle flavor of tofu and mushrooms. Add oil constantly to keep the wok well-greased and glossy as you stir-fry. Think of it as skin care for the wok.

Stir-fried Chicken with Chestnuts

This recipe lists candied chestnuts, but use fresh chestnuts if you can. Remove the bitter inner skin and fry until golden. That way, they won't crumble.

Stir-fried Tofu with Mushrooms

Ingredients (serves 4)
1 block firm tofu
Potato (or corn) starch
4 shiitake mushrooms
1/2 pack maitake (sheep's head) mushrooms
1/2 pack shimeji (clamshell) mushrooms
1/2 pack enoki mushrooms
1 clove garlic
2 red chili peppers
2 scallions
1 Tbsp sesame oil
2 Tbsp vegetable oil
1 C soup stock
A ⌐1 Tbsp sake
 ⌐1/3 tsp salt
 ⌐Dash each sugar, pepper
Soy sauce
Oyster sauce
2 Tbsp starch paste (see Reference Guide)

1. Cut tofu in half and slice each half to 2/5" (1 cm) pieces. Wipe off excess moisture. Remove stems of shiitake mushrooms and slice into 2/5" (1 cm) pieces. Remove root end of maitake and shimeji mushrooms and break up into bite-size pieces. Cut off root end of enoki mushrooms and shred.

2. Thinly slice garlic. Deseed chili peppers and slice into 2/5" (1 cm) rounds. Slice scallions diagonally to 4/5" (2 cm) pieces.

3. Dust tofu slices with starch. Heat sesame oil in a wok. Remove wok from heat, add tofu slices, and return to heat. Cook at high heat on both sides until color changes, then remove everything from wok.

4. Add vegetable oil to wok and stir-fry garlic and chili peppers being careful not to burn. Add white parts of scallions and stir-fry. Add mushrooms (except enoki), stir-fry until tender, then add enoki. Stir-fry, then remove everything from wok.

5. Pour in soup stock and return fried tofu and mushrooms to wok. Season with mixture A and cover with lid. Simmer at low heat for 2 to 3 min. Adjust flavor with soy sauce and oyster sauce, thicken sauce with starch paste, and finish with green parts of scallions.

As a general rule, cut ingredients into bite-size pieces before stir-frying.

Pat both sides of tofu dry and coat with a dusting of starch.

Remove wok from heat before adding tofu. This is a trick to adjust the heat of the wok.

Fry tofu until golden, adding sesame oil as needed, and remove from wok. Add vegetable oil and sauté mushrooms with garlic and chilies.

When other mushrooms are tender add enoki and stir-fry quickly, then remove from wok.

Finish by topping with plenty of green scallions.

Stir-fried Chicken with Chestnuts

Ingredients (serves 4)

12 chicken wings (tips removed)
12 chestnuts (candied)
2 bunching onions
   (or sub. green onions)
1 segment ginger
3 Tbsp vegetable oil
1 1/2 Tbsp oyster sauce
A ⌈ 1 Tbsp sugar
  ⎢ 1 Tbsp soy sauce
  ⌊ 1 Tbsp sake
Dash pepper
2 Tbsp starch paste
   (see Reference Guide)

1. Fill wok with 3 C water, add chicken wings and turn on heat. Boil, occasionally removing surface foam. Remove chicken and coat with soy sauce while still hot. Save remaining boiling liquid. Cut bunching onion to 2" (5 cm) pieces and thinly slice ginger.

2. Heat 2 Tbsp oil in wok. Turn off heat and arrange wings in wok. Return to heat and cook until browned on both sides, rocking occasionally.

3. Add bunching onion and ginger, pour in oyster sauce and coat. Stir-fry until fragrant and smoky. Add 1 3/4 C of reserved boiling liquid, chestnuts, and mixture A.

4. Simmer well until almost all water evaporates, approximately 15 min. Add starch to thicken sauce. Add remaining 1 Tbsp vegetable oil to finish.

Candied chestnuts can crumble easily, so handle with care.

Take boiled chicken wings from wok and pour soy sauce over while hot.

Massage soy sauce into the boiled chicken wings. They'll be hot, but you'll survive.

The oil can spatter when you add the chicken, so be careful. Cook until golden brown on both sides.

After adding oyster sauce, cook over medium heat until richly fragrant.

Add chestnuts and stir gently to allow the flavors to absorb.

Thickening the sauce traps the delicious flavors. Do it carefully, scooping up from the bottom.

AUTUMN

WINTER

Napa Cabbage Stir-fry

Blanch Napa cabbage in oil briefly, keeping the crispy texture.
Sauté chili peppers slowly, being careful not to burn.
Do these two things properly, and you've mastered this dish.

Stir-fried Pork and Daikon

Cook daikon radish and meat by blanching in oil at the same time.
You can tell the daikon is ready when the pork changes color.

Napa Cabbage Stir-fry

Ingredients (serves 4)
17 1/2 oz (500 g) Napa cabbage
4" (10 cm) bunching onion
   (or green onion)
2 red chili peppers
Oil for deep-frying
1 tsp Sichuan peppercorn
   (*hua jiao*)
2 Tbsp vegetable oil
A ┌ 1 1/2 Tbsp sugar
    1 1/2 Tbsp rice vinegar
    1 Tbsp sake
    1 Tbsp soup stock
    2 1/3 Tbsp soy sauce
    1 Tbsp starch paste
    (see Reference Guide)
  └ Dash pepper

1.   Divide Napa cabbage into leaves and stems. Cut stems to a length of 2" (5 to 6 cm) and leaves to a width of 1 1/4" (3 to 4 cm). Cut bunching onion into 2/5" (1 cm) diagonal slices. De-seed chili peppers and cut into 3 or 4 pieces.

2.   Heat oil to 350°F (180°C) and turn off heat. Add Napa cabbage and cook briefly, leaving crispy texture of stems. Transfer to a bowl of boiled water, stir well to rinse off oil, and drain.

3.   Heat oil in wok, and sauté chili peppers and Sichuan peppercorns slowly at low heat until chilies are blackened. Return Napa cabbage to wok and add mixture A and bunching onion. Stir-fry at high heat and coat with seasonings.

Cut cabbage stems along the grain first, then slice into equal-sized pieces.

To keep cabbage crispy, dip in oil just briefly and rinse by swishing around in boiling water. Speed is the key.

Sauté chili peppers and peppercorns slowly to bring out the fragrance. Don't worry if they turn black from the heat.

Return Napa cabbage to wok and add seasonings. Combine mixture A and blend before adding to wok.

Add bunching onion, thicken sauce with starch, and stir-fry well to coat cabbage thoroughly.

WINTER

Stir-fried Pork and Daikon

Ingredients (serves 4)
10 1/2 oz (300 g) daikon radish
7 oz (200 g) thinly sliced pork
A ┌ 1/3 tsp salt
│ 1 Tbsp sake
│ Dash pepper
│ 2 Tbsp starch paste
└ (see Reference Guide)
1 Tbsp vegetable oil
2 to 3 scallions
1 small nub ginger
Oil for deep-frying
1 Tbsp vegetable oil
1 Tbsp Doubanjiang (Chinese chili
paste)
B ┌ 2 tsp sugar
│ 1 tsp rice vinegar
│ 1 Tbsp sake
│ 1 Tbsp starch paste
│ (see Reference Guide)
│ 1 1/2 Tbsp soy sauce
│ 2 Tbsp soup stock
└ Dash pepper

1. Julienne daikon along the grain into 3" (7 to 8 cm) long strips. Slice pork thinly, combine mixture A and add pork to marinate.

2. Cut white parts of scallions in half lengthwise and slice thinly on the diagonal. Slice green leaves with similar thin diagonal cuts, and keep parts separate. Julienne ginger.

3. Heat frying oil in a wok to 310°F (150 to 160°C) and add daikon. Add pork and fry, breaking apart while cooking. Remove once pork turns brown. Drain oil from wok.

4. Heat vegetable oil in wok and sauté white parts of scallions and ginger. Add Doubanjiang and continue sautéing. Add fried daikon and pork, stir-fry and add green parts of scallions and mixture B. Stir-fry over high heat.

Stir oil gently with a ladle as you fry.

Cut daikon along the grain. Cut scallions on the bias.

Sautéing brings out the fragrance of the scallions and ginger and heightens the spiciness of Doubanjiang.

Add pork to the wok right after adding daikon.

Pro chefs mix their seasonings in the ladle, but at home it's easiest to mix them separately in a bowl.

Enjoy the simple sophistication of these easy-to-make sweets. They're a smooth and refreshing treat.

After enjoying a spicy feast, refresh with a simple treat.

Almond pudding, or *annin dofu*, is a popular Chinese dessert.

Evaporated milk lends it a rich flavor.

Almond Pudding

Ingredients (serves 4)
1/3 oz (10 g) leaf gelatin
1 1/4 C water
1 5/6 oz (55 g) sugar
1 can (14 oz (400 g)) evaporated milk
1 tsp almond extract
Syrup:
    2 oz (60 g) sugar
    2 C water
Mint leaves and strawberries, for garnish

1. Soften leaf gelatin by soaking in water for 15 min.
2. Place water and sugar in wok and heat until sugar melts. Continue heating until temperature reaches 175°F (80°C) and remove from heat. Drain softened gelatin. Add gelatin to hot sugar mixture and melt. Cool wok by placing in ice water. Add evaporated milk and almond extract. Mix well.
3. Strain above mixture and pour into a dish. Place in refrigerator until firm.
4. Make syrup. Bring water to a boil in wok, add sugar and simmer until melted. Cool by placing wok in ice water.
5. Scoop individual servings of almond pudding into dishes and top with syrup, strawberries, and mint leaves.

Rice Flour Dumplings with Sesame Sauce

Kneading rice dumpling flour and rolling it into little balls is actually quite fun. The dumplings are ready when they bob up to the surface of the water. Transfer them to cold water quickly.

Ingredients (serves 4)

4 1/4 oz (120 g) glutinous rice flour
   (*shiratama-ko*)
Appx. 1/2 C (125 ml) lukewarm
   water
Sesame sauce:
   2 Tbsp black sesame seeds
   1 3/4 oz (50 g) granulated sugar
   1 2/3 C (400 ml) water
   1 cinnamon stick
1 Tbsp starch paste
   (see Reference Guide)
Cinnamon stick, for garnish

1. Finely grind rice flour with a rolling pin. Transfer to a bowl and add lukewarm water a little at a time, kneading as you go. Continue kneading and adding water slowly until batter becomes the texture of an earlobe.

2. Bring water to a boil in a wok, then turn down heat. Roll dumpling dough into 4/5" (2 cm) balls and add to boiling water one at a time. Transfer dumplings quickly to cold water as soon as they bob up to the surface. Drain well.

3. Make sesame sauce. Lightly roast black sesame in a wok. Grind roasted sesame seeds using an mortar. Place water, sugar and cinnamon stick in wok and heat. When sugar melts, add ground sesame seeds and mix well.

4. Add rice flour dumplings to sesame sauce and heat. Thicken sauce with starch paste. Transfer to dishes and garnish with cinnamon stick.

Rice Flour Dumplings in Syrup

Guihua chen jiu, used in the syrup here, is a liqueur scented with sweet olive flower petals. It's very sweet and fragrant. Top with silver tree ear mushrooms to complete the elegant image.

Ingredients (serves 4)
4 1/4 oz (120 g) glutinous rice flour
  (*shiratama-ko*)
Appx. 1/2 C (125 ml) lukewarm
  water
1/3 oz (8 g) silver tree ear (snow)
  mushroom
A ⌐ 1 3/4 oz (50 g) sugar
  ∟ 2 C water
Syrup:
  ⌐ 2 3/4 oz (80 g) granulated sugar
  | 3 1/3 Tbsp *Guihua chen jiu*
  | (*bai jiu* with sweet olive flowers)
  ∟ 1 1/3 C (350 ml) water

1. Knead dough for rice flour dumplings as described on opposite page. Roll dough into 1 1/4" (3 cm) balls and press down in the middle to make an indent. Boil in water then transfer to cold water to set. Boil syrup ingredients, then let cool.
2. Reconstitute silver tree ear mushrooms in water and remove dirt. Bring mixture A ingredients to a boil briefly. Add mushrooms, simmer briefly, then chill.
3. Drain rice flour dumplings. Transfer to dishes and top with syrup and mushrooms.

TIP: *Guihua chen jiu* is said to have been made at the request of Yang Guifei (Empress Yang). Originally it was made with white liqueur, but nowadays you can find a red version, too. A light pink syrup would also be attractive.

Chill dumplings and syrup before serving. This extra step makes a big difference.

Coconut-Simmered Apples

Don't peel the apples. The bits of red scattered here and there in the dish of milk make this dish festive and attractive. Do your best to cut the apples into identical cubes.

Ingredients (serves 4)
1 apple
1 C coconut milk
2 C milk
2 1/3 oz (70 g) sugar

1.   Quarter and core apple, leaving the peel on. Dice into equal-sized 1/5" (5 mm) cubes.
2.   Heat milk and coconut milk in a wok. Add sugar and simmer until melted. Transfer to a deep dish, add apple cubes and cover with a lid. Steam in a bamboo steamer for 15 min.

When adding apple cubes, be careful to let some red skins show.

Pomegranate Jelly

**Use store-bought pomegranate juice
as well as freshly squeezed juice to enhance the color.
This sweet and sour dessert is a delight on a hot day.**

Ingredients (serves 4)
4/5 C (200 ml) store-bought 100%
   pomegranate juice
2 pomegranates
2/5 oz (12 g) leaf gelatin
1 C (250 ml) water
150 g (5 1/4 oz) sugar
3 Tbsp honey
Kiwi fruit and canned peaches,
   for garnish

1. Soak gelatin in water for 15 min. to soften. Remove pomegranate seeds, liquify in a blender and strain. Pour 4/5 C of fresh pomegranate juice in a glass.

2. Add water and sugar to wok and heat until sugar melts and reaches a temperature of 175°F (80°C). Remove from heat. Drain gelatin and melt in sugar water. Strain and transfer to a bowl.

3. Cool gelatin mixture by placing bowl in ice water. Add both fresh and store-bought pomegranate juices and honey and mix well. Pour into a flat dish and chill until firm (approximately 3 hours).

4. Cut gelatin into large bite-size slices and serve on a dish garnished with kiwi fruit and yellow peaches cut into cubes.

10 21ˢᵗ Century Recipes

These recipes are true show-stoppers. My customers always get a kick out of seeing these dishes.

Treasure-Stuffed Chicken
Recipe on page 106

Customers wait in eager anticipation
as I slice into the chicken.
What treasure will come out?
These 21st century dishes are designed
to please my customers.

Braised Spiny Lobster
with Chili Sauce
Recipe on page 107

This lobster is cooked with layers of delicious seasonings and is truly irresistible. The vegetables aren't just for decoration; enjoy them with the lobster. My policy for the 21st century is sharing delicious dishes with everyone.

Treasure-Stuffed Chicken

Ingredients (serves a large party)
1 whole chicken, gutted
   (2 1/2 to 3 1/2 lb (1.2 to 1.5 kg))
3/4 oz (20 g) Chinese ham
1 3/4 oz (50 g) pork belly
2 dried scallops
7 oz (200 g) dried shark fin, reconstituted
1 bunch of broccoli
Potato (or corn) starch
2 Tbsp vegetable oil
Soy sauce, to taste
Oil for deep-frying
A ┌ 2 C soup stock
    1 Tbsp *lao jiu* (aged rice wine)
    1 tsp sugar
    1 tsp soy sauce
    1/2 Tbsp oyster sauce
    Dash pepper
    3 Tbsp starch paste (see Reference Guide)
  └ 1/2 Tbsp chicken lard
B ┌ 3 C soup stock
    1 C Chinese white broth
    1 Tbsp sake
    1/2 tsp salt
  └ Dash pepper
5 Tbsp starch paste
2 pickled chili peppers (*pao la jiao*)

1. Rinse out chicken carefully and boil in ample water. Thinly slice Chinese ham and pork belly. Cover scallops with water and steam for 30 min. Boil shark fin to remove odors.

2. Heat oil in a wok. Add pork belly and sauté. Add soup stock from mixture A, Chinese ham, steamed scallops and boiled shark fin. Simmer at low heat for 10 min. Add remaining ingredients from mixture A and coat shark fin with plenty of sauce.

3. Stuff above mixture into boiled chicken and "cork" with a paper towel. Coat entire surface of chicken with soy sauce. Place in 350°F (180°C) frying oil and ladle hot oil over chicken until the surface turns golden brown.

4. Simmer mixture B in a separate wok for 5 to 6 min. and transfer to a large bowl. Transfer stuffed fried chicken in a large bowl and steam for 1.5 to 2 hours. Transfer steamed chicken to a dish and return soup to wok. Add starch paste to turn soup into a thick sauce and coat chicken.

5. Break broccoli into small clumps and coat with starch. Fry in oil at medium high heat and place around chicken for decoration. When serving, carve chicken into slices and garnish with *Pao la jiao*.

TIP #1: White soup is a thick soup made by simmering pork back fat in chicken broth. It is a cloudy soup with a rich and flavorful taste. *Pao la jiao* are pickled chili peppers. It's a condiment used in Sichuan Province, but if you can't find it you can use regular chili peppers cut into 2/5" (1 cm) rounds.

TIP #2: Shark fin is most likely sold dried. You can find the tail or back fins dried and left in the original shape, but these take a long time to reconstitute. For home cooking, I suggest using the version that has been dried, reconstituted, shredded, then molded into the original shape and dried again. It takes much less time to reconstitute at home. Place in hot water, cover with a lid and let sit over night. Rinse well before using. Don't forget to boil it before using it to get rid of the fishy smell.

Braised Spiny Lobster with Chili Sauce

Ingredients (serves a large party)
1 spiny lobster (*ise ebi*)
A ⌐Dash each salt and pepper
  ⌐1 Tbsp each egg white and
  └ potato starch
Cabbage, carrot, red and green
bell pepper for garnish
Oil for deep-frying
2 Tbsp vegetable oil
B ⌐1 Tbsp ginger, minced
  ⌐1 tsp garlic, minced
  ⌐1 1/2 Tbsp Doubanjiang
  └ (Chinese chili paste)
3 Tbsp ketchup
C ⌐1 C soup stock
  ⌐1 tsp each sugar and sake
  └Dash each salt and pepper
1/2 bunching onion, minced
3 to 4 Tbsp starch paste
1 Tbsp butter
1 tsp rice vinegar
Thinly grated mozzarella cheese
Powdered parmesan cheese

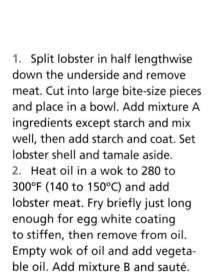

1. Split lobster in half lengthwise down the underside and remove meat. Cut into large bite-size pieces and place in a bowl. Add mixture A ingredients except starch and mix well, then add starch and coat. Set lobster shell and tamale aside.
2. Heat oil in a wok to 280 to 300°F (140 to 150°C) and add lobster meat. Fry briefly just long enough for egg white coating to stiffen, then remove from oil. Empty wok of oil and add vegetable oil. Add mixture B and sauté. Add lobster tamale and stir-fry.
3. Add mixture C and bring to a boil. Return lobster meat to wok and add minced bunching onion. Add starch paste and stir with large sweeping motions over high heat. Turn off heat. Add butter

and rice vinegar to finish. Melt better with remaining heat.
4. Spoon lobster mixture into shell, top with cheeses and bake just until toasted in a 480°F

(250°C) oven. Julienne cabbage, carrot and green pepper and dress serving plate. Place lobster on top.

Cut the juicy lobster meat into bite-size pieces. Lobster meat is so luxurious.

Sauté mixture B, add lobster tamale and stir-fry well. Stir-fry thoroughly. Add soup stock.

Add mixture C ingredients quickly one by one. Add lobster meat.

Thicken sauce with starch paste. The butter and rice vinegar added at the end complete the flavor.

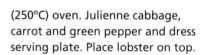

Preparing soup stock

Like Japanese *dashi* and French bouillon, Chinese cuisine also uses soup stock as a base for many dishes. You can find instant soup stock at the store, but it is better to make your own at home. The pros use different soup stocks depending on the dish, but you don't have to go that far. If you use chicken wings, it requires less preparation than making soup stock from a whole carcass, and you can still produce a rich flavor. It's an easy, all-purpose soup stock that goes well with any dish. I highly recommend trying it.

1 Ingredients: 7 1/2 C water, 8 chicken wings, green parts of 2 leeks, 1 nub ginger. Rinse chicken wings and chop ginger without peeling.

2 Fill a large wok water and turn heat to high. Add wings right away, before water starts to boil.

3 Once water is at a boil, scoop off surface foam. Carefully removing the foam will give the soup stock a refined flavor.

4 After removing foam add leek leaves and ginger. Add 4 Tbsp sake, bring to a gently bubbling boil and simmer for 30 minutes.

5 Remove any additional foam but leave chicken fat. This gives the soup stock its rich and delicious flavor. Take out wings, leek leaves, and ginger. Done!

For storage, add a dash of salt and transfer to an airtight container. Kept refrigerated it will last 2 to 3 days.

Common ingredients in Sichuan cuisine

Doubanjiang, or Chinese chili paste, is characterized by its unique spicy flavor and fragrant aroma. Chefs make good use of a wide variety of chili paste, according to degree of fermentation and level of spiciness. Well-fermented bean paste turns from red to black and the saltiness is more subdued. Sichuan pepper (*hua jiao*) is basically the Chinese version of *sansho* pepper, but it has a stronger aroma and sharper bite. The peppercorns can be used whole or ground into a fine powder known as *hua jiao fen*. *Xianglajiang* is a fragrant miso blended with chili peppers and various spices.

香辣醬 **Xianglajiang**

花椒 **Hua Jiao**

赤唐辛子 **Red Chili Peppers**

豆板醬 **Doubanjiang**

冬菜 Dong cai
(winter pickle)

This pickle, made from salted Napa cabbage, is a product of Tianjin. Along with *zha cai* (pickled mustard stem), it is one of the most well-known pickles in Chinese cuisine. It has a strong salty flavor and in some cases garlic is added. It's used as a condiment, in stir-fries, and in steamed dishes.

Chinese Pickles

Sichuan cuisine comes from Sichuan Province, situated in the middle of China's wide expanse. It's surrounded by tall mountains and far from the ocean, so seafood is a luxury item. However, the soil is rich in nutrients and agricultural products are abundant. That is why Sichuan Province is home to such a wide variety of pickles. Each has its own unique and intricate flavor. As you have seen throughout this book, these pickles play a big part in enhancing the flavor of various dishes. Please put them to good use.

搾菜 Zha cai (pickled mustard tuber)

This is one of the most popular pickles in China. It's a specialty of Sichuan Province and referred to as "Sichuan vegetable." It is made from a variety of mustard green which develops a knobby, swollen stem. The stem is dried then preserved in salt and pressed to remove any remaining water. Spices such as chili peppers and Sichuan pepper are added and then it's pickled once again.

芽菜 Ya cai (pickled mustard greens)

This pickle is similar to *zha cai* and also comes from Sichuan Province. It's made by partially drying a certain type of mustard green and pickling with five-spice powder (*wuxiangfen*) and salt. It can be found in Asian markets. Chop finely and use it to spice up meat dishes and soups.

雪菜 Xue cai (pickled cabbage)

A variety of mustard greens pickled with salt. It has a pleasantly sour taste and unique aroma and a nice crunchy texture. It adds a delicious flavor to meat and vegetable stir-fry dishes, fried rice, and soups. It's similar to the Japanese *takanazuke*.

Thank you for reading and trying these recipes!

At the time of this writing, it has been ten years since my father, Chen Kenmin, left me his restaurant chain Shisen Hanten. Over the years, I have introduced various aspects of Sichuan cuisine by writing books, making television appearances, and the like. The essence of Sichuan cuisine was impressed upon me from an early age and now my entire being is steeped in this culinary tradition. I learned everything, either directly or indirectly, from my father. To be honest, for TV I have chosen flashy, showy dishes, but inside of me there is another version of Sichuan cooking, the one mixed with Japanese cuisine. The Sichuan cuisine I grew up with at home.

Until now, I never really revealed this side of Sichuan cuisine, but in this book I went all out and included several favorite recipes from my childhood. As I was writing this book and making these dishes, my parents' faces and memories of our old house flashed before me.

Our house was on a back road in West Azabu in the Minato ward of Tokyo. Young chefs from my father's restaurant would sometimes spend the night, and I looked forward to the meals they would make on weekends. My parents were always busy, so it was my older sister who made afternoon snacks. I remember she often made the Spicy and Sour Noodle Soup I introduce in this book. I've been totally fine with very spicy foods since my early childhood. I grew up surrounded by the spices of Sichuan Province.

At night, in an attempt to make up for her absence during the day, my mother would climb into my bed and tell me stories. The stories were different every night, but she always ended with, "You'll be a great chef someday."

It was as though she were casting a spell on me, whispering those same words every night. The line, "You'll be a great chef someday," slowly but surely seeped into the core of my being. As soon as I graduated college, I worked at my father's restaurant, Shisen Hanten, starting out washing dishes. My father's apprentices were my superiors. I was trained with strict discipline and warm affection. I learned the basics of Sichuan cuisine and the systems of Chinese restaurants. I traveled to my father's hometown in Sichuan Province, and all across China and Taiwan learning new recipes.

An important lesson I learned from my father was that cuisine must change with the times and adapt to the needs of the customers. I wonder how Chinese cuisine will evolve in the 21st century. My eldest son is studying Chinese at college. I am not sure yet what his intentions are, but I can't keep from hoping. My father, my son and I all have Chinese blood in our veins, although it thins with each generation. However, I believe that our passion for the flavor of Sichuan cooking will stay the same.

In his later years my father became a Christian, and I often heard him say he was grateful "First, to God. Second, to my wife, Shoko. And third to my children and my disciples all across Japan." I, too, am full to the brim with gratitude towards my great father, my mother who supported him, towards my wife and children who support me now, and everyone at Shisen Hanten. When I was growing up my father would often say to me, "Cooking is an expression of love. The happier you are, the more delicious it becomes." On that note, I would like to leave this message for my children and for everyone who stands in the kitchen to cook:

"If you want to make delicious food, enjoy life!"

Chen Kenichi

Born in Tokyo, 1956.
After graduating Tamagawa Univer-
sity, Chen Kenichi studied Sichuan
cooking under his father, Chen
Kenmin, who is known as the father
of Sichuan cuisine in Japan. When
his father passed away, Chen Kenichi took over control of the Shisen
Hanten
also wo
While c
of genu
Kenichi
ity in th
unique
popular
appeara
His warn
can be o
book.

Photo: N
worked
Kimura,

IRON CHEF CHEN'S
KNOCKOUT CHINESE

Translation: Patricia Kawasaki
Vetting: Lisa Reilly

Published by Vertical, Inc., New York.

Originally published in Japanese as *Honnede Tsukuru
Bokuno Ryori* by Bunka Shuppankyoku, Tokyo, 2000.

ISBN 978-1-934287-46-0

Manufactured in The United States of America

First American Edition

Vertical, Inc.
www.vertical-inc.com